*A Troubled Guest*

# A Troubled Guest

## LIFE AND DEATH STORIES

# Nancy Mairs

*Beacon Press*

BOSTON

Beacon Press
25 Beacon Street
Boston, Massachusetts 02108-2892
www.beacon.org

Beacon Press books
are published under the auspices of
the Unitarian Universalist Association of Congregations.

This publication was supported by a grant from the
Project on Death in America of the Open Society Institute.

06 05 04 03 02    8 7 6 5 4 3 2 1

This book is printed on acid-free paper that meets the uncoated paper
ANSI/NISO specifications for permanence as revised in 1992.

Text design by Dean Bornstein
Composition by Wilsted & Taylor Publishing Services

Library of Congress Cataloging-in-Publication Data
Mairs, Nancy.
A troubled guest : life and death stories / Nancy Mairs.
      p.   cm
ISBN 0-8070-6248-0 (cloth)
ISBN 0-8070-6249-9 (pbk.)
1. Mairs, Nancy, date    2. Authors, American—20th century—
Biography.    3. Death—Psychological aspects.    I. Title.
PS3563.A386 Z477 2001
818'.5409—dc21        2001000958

*In memoriam*

John Eldredge Smith Jr.
September 17, 1919 – December 21, 1947

*and*

Anne Pedrick Smith Cutler
September 24, 1919 – October 28, 1998

# The Holy Longing

by Johann Wolfgang von Goethe

Tell a wise person, or else keep silent,
because the massman will mock it right away.
I praise what is truly alive,
what longs to be burned to death.

In the calm water of the love-nights,
where you were begotten, where you have begotten,
a strange feeling comes over you,
when you see the silent candle burning.

Now you are no longer caught
in the obsession with darkness,
and a desire for higher love-making
sweeps you upward.

Distance does not make you falter.
Now, arriving in magic, flying,
and finally, insane for the light,
you are the butterfly and you are gone.

And so long as you haven't experienced
this: to die and so to grow,
you are only a troubled guest
on the dark earth.

*Translated from German*
*by Robert Bly*

# Contents

# A Necessary End

BECAUSE in 1972 I learned that I have multiple sclerosis, I have reflected for more than quarter of a century on the issues that confront a person who, because of physical and/or mental deviance(s) from the nondisabled norm, tends to be viewed by society at large with the classical tragic emotions of pity and terror and deemed to be stuck in a life not worth living. A logical next step seemed to entail reflecting upon social attitudes toward the only available alternative. Although many people are quick enough to sanction death for others—in such forms as abortion, euthanasia, and capital punishment—few seem capable of contemplating their own end, or that of anyone with whom they are intimate, with anything like equanimity. I thought I might try.

Beneath my interest in death, as in disability before it, lay my desire to understand the role of affliction in perfecting human experience. Although suffering is a state often considered scandalous in modern society, a mark of illness to be cured or moral deviance to be corrected, from a spiritual perspective it is simply an element in the human condition, to be neither courted nor combated. To refuse to suffer is to refuse fully to live. Doing so leads not only to risky behaviors (self-mutilation, anorexia nervosa, and addiction all stem from an inauthentic relation to suffering) but also to an anesthesia of the soul which renders play all but impossible. In short, suffering needs to be redeemed and reincorporated into the framework we use to ascribe meaning to otherwise chaotic experience. Without death to round our little lives, they have neither shape nor sweetness nor significance.

When I was offered a contract to write a book about death, however, I replied that I might just as soon do the dying itself. I wasn't speaking figuratively or facetiously. I meant simply that I had reached the point in my crippled life where, my losses hugely outweighing my gains, death seemed less like subject matter than like an act to be got on with and out of the way. Then my condition began to suggest that I might in fact get my half-heedless wish. I might never complete such a book. I might never even get it fairly started. And I discovered that I am perhaps nowhere near as scornful of my rubbishy existence as I've often made myself out to be.

I'm willing enough to die. Some mornings I have waked weeping to find myself still alive. I no longer face the challenge of living a new day well, to which my spirit might rise, but daunting hours of struggle to accomplish the most basic tasks: capturing food on a fork and then raising it to my lips, turning the pages of a book or magazine, scratching my nose or grasping a pencil, pressing the button on my speakerphone or the joystick on my wheelchair. I have found no way to describe the attentive effort these gestures require to those who perform hundreds of them every day without notice. It used to feel like moving under water; now, like moving through aspic; one day, like moving through amber: like a prehistoric insect, not at all. Because my fatigue set in more than forty years ago, well before other symptoms of MS appeared, I've long since forgotten what unforced activity at the most mundane level feels like. I've lost the ability to formulate any plan more elaborate than wheeling from my studio to the house, retrieving my lunch from the refrigerator, and eating it—unless I upend it during the transfer, in which case the dogs will eat it while I rage. This ever-narrowing focus wears away my spirit, which feels thinner now and more likely to tear than the page on which these words appear.

My most arduous undertakings in recent years have involved the toilet, so that much of my attention each day focused on rudimentary issues: Could I transfer myself from my wheelchair to the toilet? Would I wet myself instead or in the process? Would I void completely enough to prevent the antibiotic-resistant bacteria that have colonized my bladder from proliferating into a full-blown urinary tract infection? No such luck, and so I've wound up sporting a drainage bag. Will it hold, or will it disgorge its yellow contents all over someone's new wall-to-wall carpeting? Will my bowels move today? With what kind of assistance? Because urination and defecation once formed the site for a highly charged struggle between infant and mother, and since part of mother's victory consisted in ensuring that one carried out these "duties" while thinking and speaking of them as little as possible, attention devoted to them is tainted in a way that hours spent coloring and styling one's hair or polishing one's fingernails would not be, even though these too involve managing waste matter. "Death with dignity," which has become a catchphrase now that dying can be prolonged almost indefinitely, provides a polite means of expressing what a student in a class on death and loss recently listed as her greatest end-of-life fear: "having somebody wipe my butt." The spirit eroded by effortful trivia is expended utterly in a waste of shame at these infantile concerns. I'm ready to leave them behind.

* * *

On the morning my mother decided that the few weeks her highly aggressive lung cancer could offer her would hold nothing of value to her, she mouthed to her pulmonologist, "I'm ready." Shortly thereafter, the resident covering for her primary-care physician came in. Fresh out of medical school and visibly shaken, he began to protest her decision, listing various weapons that might still be deployed. Prevented by a tracheostomy from uttering a sound, Mother regarded him implacably.

"I know this is hard for you," I said to him. "I'm sure you went into medicine to make people well, not to let them die. But you have to understand that for some of us, death is not an enemy." He couldn't understand. He went away, and we didn't see him again.

Fight or flight: a common enough response to an event that is literally unfathomable, since it extinguishes the being who does the knowing, and therefore dreadful, as any threat to our existence must be. For protection, and for comfort when protection fails, we huddle together in social formations that cope variously with the ineluctable and destabilizing fact that every individual member, regardless of station or merit, will at some point cease to be. Small wonder so many societies function as though perched on the brink of dissolution: they are, from the perspective of those members engaged in death and birth, dissolving and reforming at every instant. The corruption and imminent demise so lamented by every age in relation to its golden past is not the world's but our own. Pace the doomsayers, the cosmos seems likely to putter along all but forever, not discernibly the worse for wear; even humankind may prove surprisingly durable; but each one of us will not.

The whole of psychological development and cultural production occurs not merely in the context of but in response to the certainty of individual death: the sole absolute in the flux and welter of human experience. "Of all the wonders that I yet have heard," Shakespeare's Julius Caesar ruminates as his own end looms,

> *It seems to me most strange that men should fear*
> *Seeing that death, a necessary end,*
> *Will come when it will come.*

At least until now, death remains the ultimate necessity.

'Twas ever thus, though it may not always be. The stunning scientific advances of the twentieth century, if they continue in this one, may lead to the fulfillment of humanity's (and, as far as we can tell, only humanity's) dearest wish: to live forever. I'm not talking about the "everlasting life" of an "immortal soul" or any other such myth constructed to allay anxiety about What Comes Next (and indubitably, we reassure ourselves, something always has and therefore something will come next). I mean living on just as you live now —taking out the rubbish and the compost, changing the bedsheets on Sundays, buying new flea collars for the dogs, toasting the new year with champagne every January 1—forever. "Immortalists," people with such plans sometimes call themselves. I once knew one, quite a famous one, but he died some years back. Using nanotechnology to repair physical damage at the molecular level; freezing the body until a cure has been developed for whatever ails it, including mortality itself;

downloading "personness" onto a microchip: the schemes for self-perpetuation are many and mostly fantastical. But then, a century ago, so was swooping through the air between San Francisco and Boston, not to mention through the vacuum of space.

I feel neither doubt about the ability of scientists to invent physical immortality nor qualms about the propriety of their doing so. I've never seen the point of bleating about violations of natural law, whether these involve inserting fish genes into tomatoes to improve their shelf life or using fetal stem cells to grow new organs. After all, we eat both fish and tomatoes in some form or other. And in view of the difficulty we have dissuading adolescent girls from keeping their babies instead of permitting them to be adopted by mature infertile couples, the chance seems remote that we'll ever see, queued up outside abortion clinics, hordes of women who got pregnant solely to sell their fetuses to organ farms. New discoveries clearly and continually demonstrate our feeble grasp of natural law, which may be in itself inviolable (though certainly open to human discovery and interpretation) or, on the contrary, subject to infinite revision. One way or the other—that is, whether we've always been able to live forever but haven't learned how, or whether we've never been able to live forever until we learned how—immortality, if or when we achieve it, will be a thoroughly natural state.

What it will not be is a human state, not in any way that we might recognize those living in it as human. Not merely our physical but our psychosocial selves rest in the reality that we don't have all the time in the world. We mold our fables into life's shape: beginning, middle, end (death for tragedy, death deferred for comedy, but the reference point is the same). So too our music, which bursts forth from silence and dies away into silence again. Our paintings and photographs freeze moments out of time and suspend them against the blank space of eternity. Our relationships gain much of their piquancy from our awareness that every beloved is frail, imperfect, and subject to loss. We rear children who will bear our essence forward into a world we can never enter. Our gods differ from us in that they never die or, dying, rise again. If we lived forever, we might well go on creating, loving, worshiping, but the impetus for and the premises of these activities would be wholly alien to the ones we have now. Death makes us who we are.

And, through death, who we will never be. Here lies the reason I can't regard my death with quite the complacency I had anticipated: I find myself overcome with grief for a slew of "nevers" and "never agains." At odd moments sensory snippets streak across my memory: the sweet cold damp of certain March days in southern New England or the pungency of overheated air under pines along the summer seacoast, the shift of cooling sand under bare soles on a beach at twilight, the bob and snuffle of a newborn's head against a shoulder, a new hat at Easter in the days when everyone wore hats to church, postcoital smokes and pre-exam jitters and waltzes anytime. None of these will come again in any form but nostalgia.

True readiness, I'm learning, requires the relinquishment not just of memories but of dreams. I tally each one, the silly as well as the serious, and mourn its loss. Now I will never have a lot of money; drive a Mercedes-Benz station wagon; live in England (or Santa Monica or Manhattan, depending on my mood); receive a Guggenheim Fellowship; speak fluent

French; become a hospital chaplain; or watch my grandsons graduate from high school. Of course, I'd never have done most of these anyway, but that's not the point. The point is that, fueled by these fantasies, I've hurtled into the future, and now I'm all but out of gas. I feel an infinite and greedy curiosity. I want to know everything forever: not just what will become of the people alive now but what (if anything) civilization will look like in the next millennium, whether travel through vast spans of space and time will become possible, how long humanity will survive, how the Santa Catalina mountain range north of Tucson, Arizona, will have changed after a million years, when the sun will finally flare and gutter, whether the universe will expand forever or eventually fall in upon itself or do something altogether different that no one has yet thought of.

The future, like the past, is always a mirage, however, and so any "never" in it is only a phantom loss. Not so the present, where after long years I have finally learned to live. Here lies my only reality. I alone can cherish it. When I leave it, the entire world it embraces will vanish. This is not The End of the World. This is the end of *a* world, and billions of other worlds remain, including some in which I will have played a part, in which my absence will continue to play a part. But the transient coalescence "I" will dissolve and its world will wink out: the price (and I don't think it too steep) of its humanity.

Agreeing to write a book, no matter how reluctantly, is not at all the same as writing it, a process that always entails for me hesitation and resistance in measures far greater than I've anticipated. But a book about death? Impossible, I quickly came to believe. "Oh, you must find it so depressing," people would murmur sympathetically. But, even though I did sink into despondency early on, in association with a protracted migraine, I didn't find my subject depressing. Rather, I found it difficult, an altogether different quality, and I was daunted. In other words, I wasn't too sad to work, I was too scared to work, and I've remained in this state pretty much the whole way through. I had, to use a cliché from the vast storehouse Mother kept at her disposal, bitten off more than I could chew. Death was Too Big for me to do it justice.

I was in a humbling predicament. "The trouble with humility," my friend Rosemary Lynch used to lament every time the word cycled around in the scripture readings, "is that it's so humiliating." If it's the real thing—as I believe it was in Rosemary's case—it can come about in some pretty disagreeable ways involving the specific experiences a given individual dreads the most. My greatest bugbear dresses up as failure. I found myself dreaming up not a book but a respectable reason for breaking the contract I'd signed for a book I couldn't dream up. All things considered, suicide began to look like my most honorable option. Since this line of thought reflects the rationality of an overwrought seventh grader, which is about how old I was when I developed it, I deferred the deed.

I must have been up to something behind all this dither, because suddenly there were nine essays, and I had done what I set out to do. I had envisioned a short book made up of meditations upon death's various aspects. Having grown up in a family with a dead person, my father, at its center, I felt comfortable with the subject. I had entered the rapidly swelling cohort of people who now watched as the ranks of the generation preceding them—the generation that had stood between

them and death—thinned and withered. We now had the
same function thrust upon us by the ones coming along behind. From this position I could see that death would loom
larger and larger in my life, until it eclipsed the view altogether, and questions bubbled. Steeped in Western literature,
painting, and music all my life, I wondered how these arts
(broadly construed to include the popular and the commer-
cial) dispose their practitioners and patrons to "see"—and
not to see—death. What do artistic visions reveal about
death? About ourselves? What does it mean, for instance, that
one of the current feminine icons in the United States—em-
bodied in television and film stars, fashion models, and rock
musicians—is a very young, very sick woman, the image
of Samuel Taylor Coleridge's nightmare Life-in-Death, and
that real girls and women are dying (at the rate of a thousand
a year) to become her? Do we want our women to remain
children? And do we want our children dead?

Through such subtle cultural forces we develop and dis-
seminate shared attitudes and behaviors that may impoverish
us. As one of life's major events, death might be prepared for
as carefully, and conducted as ceremonially, as a wedding or
the birth of a child; but generally it is not. What are the emotional and spiritual consequences of ignoring or denying
the only outcome our lives can possibly have? What might be
the effects of living in a state of preparedness? How can we
achieve awareness of life's end without spoiling all our fun?
And when death takes from us someone we love, how can we
mourn most fruitfully? Contemporary attitudes about mental
hygiene suggest that grief is a diseased state to be gotten over
rather than a ceaseless process of coming to terms with rup-

ture; the proliferation of "grief and loss" counselors reinforces this sense of pathology. Might bereavement be viewed in ways that would make it wholesome, however painful?

Beyond the ways that each individual relates to death lies the vast territory—wasteland, I'm almost inclined to say—of ways in which we turn mortal matters over to society at large. Medical ethics and the legal system have struggled, not altogether successfully, to keep up with the consequences of advances in medical technology. Where does the power over life and death really rest: in the courts? the operating room? individual conscience? God? How do the decisions we make about such matters affect the quality of our own and others' lives? Is killing—whether in mercy or in reprisal—ever justified? A friend, a member of the Coalition of Arizonans to Abolish the Death Penalty, once gave me a bumper sticker reading, "Why do we kill people who kill people to show that killing people is wrong?" Well, why *do* we? And why do so many of those who support the death penalty also belong to the right-to-life movement? How can they have it both ways? My friendship with two people who actively oppose capital punishment—one whose son was on death row until his sentence was commuted, the other whose daughter was abducted and murdered—have kept these issues alive in my thoughts, as has my correspondence with several death-row inmates at the Arizona State Prison, one of whom has now been executed.

Whichever route my ruminations take, one question always runs beneath them: What next? Eschatological discourse can tend toward the airy-fairy or the apocalyptic, but at bottom most of us carry around quite commonsensible notions of what happens to us after we die. These are pure constructs, of course, cobbled together from whatever sources a given culture makes available to provide a means of thinking about the truly unthinkable: that each of us will one day depart this life in some mixture of faith and fear. I have friends who, having enjoyed privileged and productive lives, are firmly convinced that their loved ones have gone on to a perfected version of this world, there meeting up with old chums and enjoying endless rounds of golf while they wait for the rest of the gang to come along and join them. Others need not perfection of but rescue from the world. A death-row inmate, who has found no joy in his world, reassured me about his impending execution: "I am glad the process is proceeding on, as far as I am concerned I have no problem dieing, I am Christian, and I have complete trust and faith in the Lord Jesus Christ, I do strongly believe in the hereafter, in fact I am certain of it." With God's forgiveness he will really live at last. Nothing at all awaits still other people (though not nearly so many as you might think, since numerous surveys have estimated that more than 80 percent of us in the United States believe in an afterlife of some sort). Then there are those like me, who, feeling continuous with the rest of the matter and energy in the cosmos, expect to endure forever but not in any form that my present consciousness could comprehend. No friends, no golf games, no glory, but no annihilation either. What next? I dunno. Surprise me.

These and myriad other questions posed themselves readily enough in the abstract. I neither live nor work there, however, but in the too, too solid flesh whose frailty renders them hu-

manly impossible not to ask. Thus in this book I do not attempt to address these questions directly but rather to permit
responses to them to unfold in the context of life experience.
As always, I write from the particular perspective my circumstances dictate: as a cripple; a Catholic grounded in liberation
theology; a daughter, wife, sister, and mother; a depressive; a
feminist. Certain significant lacunae—I do not, for instance,
treat mass death either natural (through earthquakes, floods,
volcanic eruptions, and the like) or political (through war
or genocide)—occur because, lacking direct experience of
them, I am the wrong person to discuss them in the detail
they merit.

I remain a homely writer. For most of my life but especially
over the past ten years, ever since my husband, George, developed stage-IV melanoma and survived, I have lived on intimate terms with the personal complexities that dying pre-
sents. In a very real sense, and entirely without design, death
has become my life's work. There was George, and through
his illness the many members of our Living with Cancer support group. There were the diabetic maiden lady across the
street with her cat Sally, and the widower in the little house on
the corner under the jacaranda tree whose only child worked
in a city too far away to permit frequent visits, and our ninety-
five-year-old friend, childless and widowed for nearly fifty
years, who no longer recognized us reliably but charmed us
till the end. Aging uncles and aunts began to go, and then parents, and then, against all natural principles, a child.

In their usual manner, as separations and losses mounted,
my thoughts turned to writing. Having departed the academy
years ago, I wasn't about to embark on a thanatological trea-

tise. Nor was I eager to undertake an exhaustive study of the American way of death, its practices and peculiarities, since quite a few of these have been done, and done well, already. Some such works are listed at the end of this book in the Resources section. I certainly intended to be neither lugubrious nor inspirational. Awash in the sensational silliness that spews from their bookstores, their television sets, sometimes even their pulpits, people seem eager to be addressed quietly, with affection and good humor, about issues charged with personal significance. I have written these meditations to them, the ones looking for some sustenance tarter and tougher than chicken soup—grapefruit, maybe, or rhubarb. Because I look for enlightenment as much in the compost heap as in the lilies of the field, I view death with equal measures of reverence and humor, and I hope everybody gets to laugh out loud at least once.

Writing is an almost metabolic process for me, through which, in scrutinizing my own experience and relating it to the experiences of others, I incorporate myself into the human family. In one of the first essays I ever wrote, I said of my life story that there is not an original word in it. I have not changed my mind on this point (though I have on a good many others) in the nearly twenty years since. No matter how wildly they may differ in the details, the trajectories of our lives tend to replicate one another. The riddling sphinx of Thebes knew this. Shakespeare's saturnine Jacques knew it. Across time and across cultures, people who reach a point in their lives analogous to mine find themselves confronted with death more and more frequently until, one day, they come smack up against their own. If you have any reason for reading my story (and obviously I hope you will find one), do so not for its originality but for the ways it resonates with your own. Because I have a certain facility with language, what I'm good for is putting our stories into words. It is my way of taking hands in the dark.

Hold tight!

# Death with Father

AMONG Mother's things, my sister Sally and I have found a
worn black album with brittle tan pages, inscribed

July 3, 1942
San Francisco, California
Ensign and Mrs. John Eldredge Smith, Jr.

inside the front cover, containing mostly snapshots, as well as
a few clippings and other memorabilia, from the earliest part
of her five-and-a-half-year marriage to our father. The glue
having dried out long since, we confront something of a jig-
saw puzzle with most of the pieces the same size and shape and
only an occasional caption to guide us. Although familiarity
with the narrative the pieces relate enables us to work with
some confidence, an occasional face leaves us blank, and we
have nowhere to turn for guidance. The principals in this
drama are all now dead or—when we come to baby pictures—mute. Although I am the baby—Sally not even born
yet—the pictures were taken before my conscious memories
began. Over the years, I have looked at this record any number of times while Mother told me the story. But, I think now
that Mother can never answer my questions again, I never listened quite closely enough.

As we sort and remount the photos, the likeness to which
my eye is most drawn is, as always, my father's. "How handsome he was!" Sally exclaims, an observation that has been

made so many times as to have been reduced to a family cliché. Still, it's true. A short, muscular man with dark, close-
cropped hair, he appears either formally in the uniform of a
naval officer or more casually in a white T-shirt and pleated
trousers or, all but naked, in a swimming suit. The pictures
here, like all the others in my possession except for some Ko-
dachrome slides taken on Guam, are black and white, but I
can get a rough sense of his coloring by glancing in the mirror, since I turned out to be the "Smith" child as Sally turned
out to be the "Pedrick" one: his eyes slate blue, his complexion clear and high-toned. His voice, I can remember, was
deep and resonant.

You can see that my parents were crazy about each other,
both from their expressions and from the coy captions Mother
penned in her upright black handwriting. They had met
the summer they were thirteen at Daddy's family home in
Kennebunkport, Maine, where Mother's recently divorced
mother had taken rooms in search of relief for her migraine
headaches; a group snapshot from that time opens the album.
They weren't childhood sweethearts. In high school Mother
went steady with a boy whom she continued to date at least
part of the time she was at Wheaton College and he at Geor-
gia Tech. But during the year Daddy spent at Harvard while
he waited for an appointment to the Naval Academy, he initiated a correspondence, and from then on they kept in touch
and saw each other whenever the regimented life of a mid-
shipman and a young naval officer permitted. For the next
sixty years, whatever other possessions may have been lost or
jettisoned along the way, his letters accompanied her from
one home to the next.

Until the past few days I had never read these letters, though I've had some in my possession for twenty years. One of them, Mother said, was so sexually explicit that she'd be embarrassed to have it read in her lifetime; and so I could not in good faith look at them until she died. It turned out that the ones she'd given me, which I thought were all that existed, had come from their relatively chaste college years. But after her death we turned up a cache—hundreds and hundreds of sheets covered in Daddy's angular hand—spanning the decade 1937–1947. Now I've read them through, and although all are amorous and a few are a little risqué, none strike me as remotely pornographic. Either her sensibilities were more delicate than mine, or she went through them at some point and removed whatever seemed too private to share.

No matter. Whenever my parents were separated, Daddy wrote to Mother almost every night, and she kept every sheet. Often he dreamed of the immediate or long-term future they would share when they were finally reunited, but in his wildest fancies he could never have foreseen that his words would be read one day in the dining room of a stucco house in Tucson, Arizona, by a woman now twice as old as he would ever get to be, even older than his own mother was when he knew her, a woman with silvering hair who slumps in a wheelchair, a bag of urine strapped to her leg, her limp fingers scrabbling at one yellowed sheet after another as, reconstructing the life of a man she scarcely knew, she hears—for the first time in her adult life—her father's voice.

A few photos from their courtship have been pasted into the album, and a handful more lie among the loose material shoved inside the back cover, but the fullest account of this

period lies in the letters. I wish that it weren't monologic—
that Mother's letters had survived to give it clarity and balance—but there are just a few written at the end of that period. These recount a nicely dramatic moment. The Naval
Academy class of 1942 was graduated and commissioned on
December 8, 1941, and Daddy was stationed aboard the
U.S.S. *Tennessee* on the West Coast. Although he was forbidden to marry for the foreseeable future, they clearly had
begun to talk—or at least banter—about such a step. The
indefinite postponement, the country-wide separation, and
above all the anxiety of never knowing where he was (and
he was, among other places, in the Coral Sea) clearly tried
Mother's good nature. On March 29, 1942, she wrote: "I
wouldn't marry you for love nor money as long as you consider marriage a thing we 'might try.' When I step off, it will
be for life, barring unforeseen catastrophe—and not with the
idea that there's a way out if need be. But then, you say you
*know* I have no such desires, or have I? You're asking me? I
should tell you, when I've never been seriously proposed to!"

The following week, when the ban on marriage imposed
when his class graduated was suddenly lifted, she received her
proposal in a brief late-night telephone call. Don't answer me
now, Daddy told her, but wait until you receive the letter I've
written. Scribbled in pencil on hotel stationery with the let-
terhead ripped out for security reasons and posted air mail/
special delivery, the letter begins, "First of all: Will you
marry me now?" and goes on to delineate the reasons she
would not want to do so. She would have to leave her home
and family and job to cross the country and check in at a
strange hotel in a strange city, where she might or might not

find him. If he was there, she must settle for a simple ceremony and a forty-eight-hour honeymoon, after which she would have to take up, without much money, an itinerant and largely solitary life. "Remember," he cautioned, "that you will have a husband who may go away and not come back at any time."

She replied by return post: "I didn't know it was humanly possible for one girl to be as happy as I am right now." "I had made up my mind Monday night just after you called and I recovered my balance," she wrote, but she'd waited for his letter as he'd asked. Nothing in it dissuaded her in the face of her love for him. "I seem to have the courage to face both" — moving around and being alone. "You reminded me that I will have a husband who may go off and not come back," she told him. "I know that. But remember that I will have had you for a husband" — no matter how briefly — "and may we laugh at this thought when we're grandparents!" She was firm: "I am yours forever." And she was.

The album begins in earnest with their wedding, on May 24, 1942, at the First Congregational Church in San Francisco. Although Mother settled in Long Beach, which became my birthplace, they were also posted briefly in Bremerton, Washington, and Washington, D.C., photos and ticket stubs attest. But they were apart for weeks and months at a time. On the whole the wartime letters make for dull reading, since Daddy could divulge no detail of his whereabouts or activities. Night after night he told Mother nothing but how smart and sweet and lovely and desirable she was, how capably she handled their affairs, how he longed to return and take her in his arms; and I'm sure she never grew tired of this tune.

A few poses of Mother pregnant are followed by some of Daddy holding me at five weeks, still scarcely bigger than a doll and with quite an extraordinary shock of straight black hair dwarfing my crumpled face. At sea for the final months of Mother's pregnancy, Daddy had awaited the birth of his son ardently, and he didn't learn that he had a daughter instead until I was two weeks old, but the letters never voice the least disappointment that I—and later my sister—weren't boys. When Sally went to kindergarten, they planned to have two more children, and surely a son would come then. At one point in the letters he refers to Mother's wishing that they hadn't had any children so soon, and I feel wounded and guilty, a trespasser into a life that might have been happier without me, but at the time of my birth, I seemed nothing but welcome. "Our baby," he calls me in the letters, "our Nancy," and for the first time it occurs to me that he actually actively loved me. I've reasoned that he did, of course, knowing how I feel about my own children, but I've never apprehended so immediately his boundless affection.

Apparently, nude sunbathing was recommended for infants, for in several snapshots I lie in my carriage looking rather like a frog ready for dissection. Last comes a sequence in which I gleefully drop a small stuffed panda out of my wooden playpen. I appear to be about a year old, and we would have moved by then to Troy, New York, so that Daddy could earn his bachelor's and master's degrees in civil engineering at Rensselaer Polytechnic Institute (RPI). His eyesight wasn't keen enough to permit him to remain a line officer; and in the havoc wreaked by war, the military would require experts who could supervise the restoration of the infrastructure and services that "civilization" demanded. For the next two years he pursued with due diligence the arcana of architectural planning principles, diesel engines, heating and ventilation, highways and airports, and the like.

Perhaps the fact that Sally was conceived and born during this time explains why the remaining pages of the album contain no more snapshots, since the project may have required more time than the frazzled mother of infants and toddlers could spare. Huge numbers of photos survive from subsequent years, but faded and hopelessly curled, they rest in boxes, bags, folders, and envelopes. Sorting out after Mother's death, just as we'd be sure we must have found them all, someone would unearth a batch in a bottom desk drawer or the back of the linen closet and let out a groan. Not until she traveled after retirement did she return to keeping meticulous photographic records. For Christmas the year before she died, she gave each of us children an album assembled laboriously from her vast, uncataloged hoard. We were charmed to have these evocative and often funny visual biographies, but I don't think any of us took her act as premonitory.

Puzzlingly, the final item glued into the album dates from some years later than the last snapshots: a newspaper clipping, dated February 17, 1948, recounting Daddy's death on Guam and describing his funeral in Exeter, New Hampshire, and burial at the Arundel Cemetery in Kennebunkport. I try to imagine what was going through the mind of the woman — slight, stony, staring through the smoke of a Chesterfield, scissors and paste pot beside her — who fixed the clipping there. Since she no longer mounted family mementoes, was this the only place she could think of for preserving it? But why, since the album had fallen into disuse, did she have it at hand at all? Had she dug it out of her mother's attic, where it must have lain in storage while we lived in the Pacific, to revisit the days when her future had seemed not just possible but perfect? Had she fixed the clipping there as a bitter comment upon the fate of her youthful dreams?

By the time he'd graduated from RPI, they hadn't had much time left, and they spent a good deal of that apart. While he shipped out, in May 1946, to become the Public Works Officer on Moen in the Western Pacific atoll of Truk, she took their two little girls back to her mother's home in Massachusetts until he could send for the three of us. The island had to be cleared of Japanese soldiers; dependent housing had to be constructed and furnished; a seaplane beached on a coral reef, and the generator shack burst into flames; shipments arrived slowly or not at all; weeks stretched into months. When at last (no earlier than November) her travel was approved, she packed us aboard a plane to San Francisco and a ship to Guam. From there a military plane flew us down to Truk, where we lived for a few months before being transferred to Guam. Our life there is captured in a couple of dozen snapshots, the few colored slides, and my own memory, which had become persistent and retentive though perhaps not entirely reliable (whose is?). Still, the floor plan of our Quonset hut sketched in one of the last surviving letters is almost exactly as I would have drawn it.

On the other side of the world from home, Mother and Daddy began the life they had deferred for so long. As a family, we went to church and birthday parties and boat trips and picnics on the beach. With an ample supply of babysitters and the money to afford them, with no studying to eat into their leisure as it had in graduate school, they often ignored Sally's tempestuous wails and went to cocktail parties, dined at the officers' club or with friends, played bridge, or watched the latest film shipped out from the mainland. They would have been to some such affair—a Christmas party, no doubt—on December 21, 1947. Afterward, having taken the babysitter home, he drove his jeep over an embankment. A nurse who chanced to see the accident rushed to him, but he was already dead. Because she didn't believe the impact severe enough to have killed him, the doctors speculated that he had had a cerebral hemorrhage, perhaps dying before he ever left the road, but no autopsy was performed. What did it matter? Having survived the war, he must have seemed home free, their future stretching before them as azure and golden as the Pacific they woke to every morning. Now he had gone off and not come back. They were twenty-eight.

With the courage and competence Daddy had praised time and again, Mother reversed the journey she had made with such anticipation the year before. This time we flew to San Francisco and took the train across the country, arriving in— fittingly enough—the dead of winter. She settled us in a spacious if slightly seedy duplex just a few blocks from Daddy's parents' home in Exeter, New Hampshire. There, with little money but boundless will, she set about constructing for her daughters a life as secure and privileged as she could make it. That emotional privation lay at its core, tainting every delight with longing and loss, could hardly be blamed on her. She was the more deprived. No one ever knew how she did it. Early in February, when her sister married one of Daddy's school chums, Mother put on a blue gown and served as matron of honor. Less than two weeks later, she attended Daddy's funeral. No one ever saw her cry.

If only she had cried, all our lives would have been different.

Nowadays, a woman and children tragically abandoned in this way might well be deluged with offers of counseling from various quarters: the navy, the American Red Cross, the funeral director, the minister, the children's school. So commonplace is this service that, plugging "bereavement counseling" into an Internet search engine, I am told that more than a million Web pages address the subject in terms of every imaginable contingency. If I looked hard enough, I might even find a resource for mourning the demise of a favorite potted plant, a small but not negligible loss. In the mid–twentieth century, however, psychological assistance was still associated with "psychoanalysis," and anyone forced to resort to it was considered at least sexually perverse and probably downright nuts. It was not the sort of thing you'd offer to a nice young widow and her innocent little girls and certainly not the sort of thing she'd accept. She could—and did—manage on her own, thank you very much. Spiritual counseling, in the form of calls by the minister, would have been socially acceptable, and perhaps Mother received these—politely, without doubt—but I can't imagine her baring her soul to the Reverend Mr. Martin or anybody else. She'd have smiled her tight, bright smile and assured him that she and the girls were getting on just fine.

And really we were. Mother enrolled me in the Exeter Day

School, which was very small and staffed by lively, young single women who made every activity—whether folk dancing, tapping trees and boiling maple syrup, banging together a bookcase, or reciting John Masefield's "Sea Fever"—seem a bit of a lark. When it came time for Sally to join me, Mother worked off part of our tuition as school secretary, remaining reassuringly close at hand. We clung to her with a tenacity born of well-founded terror that she might abscond without warning, and she must sometimes have felt stifled by the hot little bodies pressed against her, by the watchful eyes darkening if she strayed away, beaming at her return. She spent countless hours in our company, reading us stories and poems, playing our children's records, listening to our prattle, cooking the pancakes we insisted on every Sunday night, nursing us through earaches, tonsillectomies, measles, chicken pox, and dabbing Merthiolate onto one wound or another and kissing it to make it all better. She must have thought that if she had to listen to "Tubby the Tuba" just once more, she'd scream. But she didn't scream. She was sometimes angry. She once put me to bed without any supper because I'd ignored her whistle calling me home. But she never took her grief and loneliness and boredom out on us.

To relieve her from relentless solitary child-rearing, Daddy's parents, Garm and Pop, had us spend the summers at their beach cottage. Aunt Nancy and Uncle Sam and their first one, then two, then three, then four little boys came, too. Once in a while, exotic Aunt Sallie breezed in from Manhattan, and a couple of times Uncle Bill, crippled by polio, brought his growing family up from Florida. Garm hired a teenage girl as a mother's helper, giving the adults assistance with the drudgery of housekeeping and child care and freeing them in the evenings to go out. Mother must have relished the opportunity to lie on the beach, play bridge, listen to Red Sox games, and simply chat with peers in addition to two very bright but often silly little girls. One of the advantages of the arrangement for us was that we lived for weeks at a time in the company of men. These were alarming creatures—deep-voiced and boisterous and teasing—but they were fond of us, the only girls in our generation for many years, and we learned to trust them.

Always at Memorial Day and at least once during the summer we also went to Kennebunkport, where rafts more of Daddy's family lived at least part of every year. Here, too, noisy and affectionate teasing abounded. And here my father remained alive more vividly than anywhere else, in the stories that get told and retold whenever the several generations of a family gather around the kitchen table or on the wisteria-draped porch or out under the apple tree to catch a bit of a breeze. Daddy was spoken of everywhere, naturally, if the occasion arose. Whether out of a desire for privacy or uncertainty how to deal with children's grief, Mother seldom initiated conversations about him with us girls, although she always responded to our comments and questions. But daily life, of necessity, unfolds in the present, where Daddy no longer lived. The stories recounted at the 'Port tended to be old ones, and Daddy, as the eldest of four, tended to figure prominently—and sometimes hilariously—in many of them. I relished every telling.

When I say that Daddy no longer "lived" in the present, I do not mean that he wasn't an entity in it, because he dwelled in our midst every moment. Time and again, people have told me that after the death of someone they loved, people—even people they considered friends—muttered hasty condolences or none at all and never referred to the dead one again. "As if," my friend Martha says in vexation, "as long as I don't hear Jack's name, I'll forget that he's dead." As if the dead one were a stone cast into a still pond: a small eruption of shimmering drops, a subsidence, a ring of ripples radiating from the point of entry, and then the glassy surface again, unrent, unruffled. But bereavement doesn't work in this way at all. Nature abhors a vacuum, the saying goes. I don't know whether it is scientifically true, but it certainly applies to human nature. Although reminders may occur less frequently over time, and grief may alter in character and intensity, no moment arrives, ever, when the dead one vanishes altogether from the consciousness of those who knew him. His very absence has become a fixed and insistent presence in their lives.

"Dead one" seems a clumsy and not especially accurate locution for the entity I have in mind, but my dictionary leaves me at a loss for a better one. "Corpse" won't do, since it refers specifically to the body, which is around for only a short while. "Deceased," with its Latinate origin, has a professional ring: it's the sort of formal word that slides off the tongues of lawyers, doctors, and funeral directors without reminding them that a corpse might be involved. Both "the dear departed" and "the loved one" lend themselves to irony of the sort that the writer Evelyn Waugh employed to devastating effect. Anyway, "departed" is the exact opposite of what I mean; my point is that the dead one *remains*, however transformed. It is thus, although materially without life, not precisely dead. "Spirit" might work for those of us who are mystically inclined, but to secularists the term suggests material for yet another spooky movie.

The absence of a lexicon for speaking conversationally about people who have died reveals the alienation from death most people feel, I think. If, by referring readily to our dead ones, we give them a place among us, then we must acknowledge that where they live, we too will live one day: in the cemetery, in the memories of those who knew us, in their stories and prayers and imaginations, but never again in the consciousness we occupy today. If they die, we die, too. Better not to remind ourselves. Better not to give them a name.

I consider myself fortunate that, although no one spoke obsessively about Daddy, references to him were neither discouraged nor forbidden and that his death was treated as a sad but natural feature of our lives. I don't mean to imply, however, that we did not suffer as a consequence of it, because we did. We'd have been monsters if we hadn't suffered in our various ways. I cannot articulate from experience the anguish of the wife who lived for fifty-one years after her young husband's death, of the mother who lost her firstborn, of the siblings whose elder brother suddenly left the field of their striving uncontested, although I can now identify some of the damage they sustained. I can report with confidence that death constitutes abandonment, however unwilled, and that abandonment by a parent marks a child as no other event can. In our bereavement, Sally and I clung together like—well, like the little children we were, each seeking solace from a nameless dread that did not destroy but certainly darkened our every delight. This took a different form for each of us, not just because we were temperamentally individual but because I could remember Daddy and she could not. Thus she lost something but she can't say for sure just what; and she has devoted much of her life to ensuring that such a disaster never recurs. Remembering a man who loved me and then went away, I dread desertion; as is often the case when an intense relationship is disrupted early on, I've been depressed since I was a child. While Sally remains vigilant, orderly, in control, I collapse into lassitude under the weight of my own despair.

I don't believe that Daddy's death led to all our divergences, of course. We were sisters, not clones: the blonde child and the dark, the round and the angular. She was given to gusts of temper like summer squalls; I, to long slow sulks. Plump and giggly, she was the sort of child people caught up and cuddled; to me, they talked. She went to daunting lengths to be the good child, she has admitted to me; self-absorbed and inclined toward hysterics, I could never figure out just what others wanted of me. We each half-coveted the other's attributes, I suspect, and we'd have been no better satisfied if we'd gotten them. These are our biological and behavioral realities. Daddy's death did not confer but complicated them.

As a further complication, we were the daughters of an abandoned daughter. Mother's father had forsaken his children twice, first divorcing my grandmother when Mother was eleven, then shooting himself dead about a decade later. In both instances the circumstances were the seamiest possible; and in their responses Mother and her sister, who had a brother between them, diverged far more sharply than Sally and I. Whereas Aunt Jean remained in lifelong thrall to a glamorous figure capable of loving no one, not even himself, Mother's fury at her father—the kind reserved for only our most beloved—remained palpable, though largely unacknowledged, throughout her life. And then her own husband decamped, leaving her children fatherless. True, the circumstances couldn't have resembled each other less. Such distinctions are drawn by reason, however. At the deeper, feeling level, history repeated itself, stirring up that raw and unresolved fury that could never be admitted, rendering her especially ill suited to guide us through our own rage and grief. She could not even afford to recognize these qualities in us lest they overwhelm her. She shut down emotionally, and in our own ways so did we.

At some level she sensed her incapacity, I think, and felt guilty whenever we behaved in ways that suggested we were in distress. She probably assumed that she was botching the lonely job of rearing her fatherless girls. I have no way of knowing whether she'd have benefited from bereavement counseling, but she certainly needed reassurance that all children go through bad patches, which most mothers imagine that they could deflect if only they were better informed, quicker to praise, more vigilant, less impatient, stricter or more lenient—the list of inadequacies, though it varies from woman to woman, tends to be long. Without question, we developed problems attributable to our early loss, but if Daddy had lived, other events would have triggered other difficulties to be coped with, as they must do if any child is going to develop into a normally good-humored and resilient adult.

A death in the family creates social as well as emotional complexities. Even Mother's iron grip on her feelings occasionally slipped. Exeter was not a large metropolis, and most of the people Mother encountered knew of her tragic loss. Most, but not all. At a gathering one evening, she once confessed to me, a woman with whom she was speaking craned her neck this way and that, chirping, "I don't believe that I've met *Mr.* Smith? . . ."

"No, and you're not likely to," Mother responded blandly, "because he's dead." Their chat did not continue. She was seldom rude, but she must have grown sick to death of such inquiries, as well as the apologies and condolences, with the whiff of condescension these inevitably bear. Dealt a rotten hand, she generally played it with style.

As long as we lived in Exeter, everyone I knew, even my classmates, seemed aware that my father was dead. No one outside my family ever mentioned him to me. When I was nine, we moved to a Massachusetts village where we knew no one, and I began to learn the awkward art of "getting acquainted." To my chagrin, this appeared to involve questions about family. A little later, I would meet a couple of girls whose mothers were divorced; but in the fifth grade, as far as I could determine, everybody had—and talked about—both parents. When asked about my father, I said he was in the navy. This equivocation—something short of a bald-faced lie, I reasoned, since he would still be in the navy if only he hadn't died and then I'd be somewhere far away from these embarrassing questions—had the virtue of explaining his absence should anyone go so far as to ask me to produce him. Why his deadness should mortify me so I can't now recall, but it simply never occurred to me to answer, "He's dead." There was never any humiliating exposé of my prevarication, but before long the questions stopped, so I suppose the truth got around as it does (along with the lies) in a small town.

In adolescence I swung the other way, exploiting my father's early death for the attention it drew to my sensitive and poetic nature. At the same time I began, not unusually for a girl abandoned young, to develop romantic attachments—"crushes," they were called, but they were too obsessive for such a light-hearted word—to older men. In retrospect, I can see that my behavior was flirtatious, even provocative, and I am lucky that the objects of my adoration were all too principled (or too bored) to succumb to my clumsy but heartfelt blandishments. By then I was seriously depressed, though still several years away from diagnosis and treatment, and a sexual relationship with one of these daddies might easily have driven me to suicide. Along the way, I grew desperate to be married and—in another stroke of sheer good fortune—entangled a young man in my scheme who has been my husband for thirty-eight years. From the first, George reminded Mother of my father.

I continued to act out sexually until I was a decade older than Daddy was when he died. Interestingly, the men who had once been older were now younger than I. Then, at long last, my depression was successfully medicated so that I could relinquish all that silliness and "get a life," as my children might have said. (This turn sent my husband into a tailspin that played out in a prolonged sexual affair of his own.) Despite the strain these and other bad behaviors put on our marriage, I never seriously considered divorce. I had two children, and I was determined that they would grow up in a two-parent household. Whatever deprivations marred their psyches, they would have a resident father; they could count on unconditional love from more than one fragile source; they would learn to accommodate our very different styles; and I would have a partner to share the most vital but also the most difficult work of my life. With ample counseling and even more goodwill, we became and remained a family.

Today when I visit college classes, I ask the students whether they've taken a course in the theory and practice of parenthood; they look a little affronted, as though I'd suggested they had time to waste on trivialities. In raising the question, however, I'm not so much recommending that such a course ought to be required for graduation (though I happen to like the idea) as revealing the general social attitude toward child-rearing even among our "best and brightest": that any idiot can carry it out with less training than is needed to operate a motor vehicle. Often brought up amid domestic chaos themselves, these young people will casually reproduce, in or out of wedlock, and rear their children (or, in the case of noncustodial parents, permit them to be reared) with a single parent, reasoning (or praying) that the kid'll do just fine as long as he's got his own Gameboy and cell phone and maybe a morning dose of Ritalin just to be on the safe side.

As the child of an absent father, reared by the most conscientious mother imaginable, I can attest that even though under such circumstances one may well grow up "just fine," ruptured relationships have lasting consequences. For years after I was married, for example, whenever George returned home later than I'd anticipated, I'd greet him hysterically: "Where the hell have you been!" An only child who had never been accountable at home to anyone but his parents, he'd respond with the sullenness of an adolescent out past his curfew. More than ten years passed before I began—I can still see myself that day, pacing to the dining room window, staring out into the empty street, a cigarette fuming between my fingers—to examine the images that triggered my panic every time: the auto spinning out of control and smashing into a pole, the lights, the sirens, the murmuring bystanders, George's body mangled, even lifeless, on a gurney. And suddenly I recognized in myself not the looming mother of a James Thurber cartoon, not the raving harpy both of us had often taken me to be, but a little girl whose father had gone off on a mundane errand and never returned. With this insight in mind, George learned to telephone me if he is going to be late, thus quieting the panicky little girl. In return, I must accept his explanation with as little question or complaint as possible so that I don't trigger the truculent little boy in him, a behavior at which I've become so adept that he was able to carry on that lengthy extramarital affair without discovery.

As time passed, my relationship to Daddy changed. Early on, I indulged in the magical thinking, also characteristic of adopted children, that if only Daddy were around, he would rescue me from my mother's meanness and my life would be as delightful as a child of my obvious merit deserved. By the time I entered adolescence, the fairy godfather had been transformed into a vigilant critic. "Your father would be so proud!" I'd be told whenever I excelled. Or (more often, at least in my memory) when I'd fallen short, "What would your father think?" And most coveted of all: "You're just like your father!"

This last comment hung on me heavily because, unlike his

survivors, Daddy became and remained perfect in every way. That's the grace death bestows on each of us, at least if we've behaved with a modicum of decency in life: memory tends to blur and burnish our faults, and since we're no longer around to transgress anew, we enter into incorruptibility. For someone as skeptical as I am of heaven (though I like the Talking Heads' notion that nothing ever happens there), here is an afterlife about which I have no doubt. Dying young, Daddy had had less time than most to besmirch his reputation anyway, and I have wondered more than once how he might have matured. A few Christmases ago, upon opening a photographic card from the family of one of his cousins, a retired naval officer about my age, I caught a glimpse of my father in middle age: stocky, still handsome, his dark hair going gray. Because my grandmother and her sister married first cousins, this vision was not genetically implausible. But there are other, darker genetic probabilities as well. His father and at least one of his siblings were alcoholics, and his letters abound with enthusiasm for drinks and smokes. In a career where promotion depended in part on sociability, played out at countless cocktail and dinner parties where one (or one's pretty wife or mannerly daughters) might catch the eye and stick in the mind of an admiral one might never see in the course of duty, might he not have found himself awash on seas of more than salt water?

As one of those daughters, I have also wondered how differently my life might have unfolded had it been shaped by a live and not a dead father. Since, having graduated eighth in his class and attained the rank of lieutenant commander well before his death, he would likely have become an admiral himself, my circumstances would have been more prosperous but less stable. His letters reveal him as a strict disciplinarian with high standards. Under his thumb, would I have become more docile—or less? Specifically, would the two most formative undertakings of my life—my resistance to the Vietnam War and my conversion to Roman Catholicism—have taken place? I suspect not. And who would I have become without them? The answers to questions like these, lying along other branches of the infinite universe, are intrinsically unknowable. I ask them only to suggest that the constructive power of the absent father equals that of a living man, however different the outcomes may be.

For better or worse, I was never the admiral's daughter, and gradually I freed myself from the compulsion to be worthy of my imaginary father. I approached, achieved, exceeded the age he was when he died, and he was no longer the omnipotent figure I could never live up to but my contemporary, a man with whom I might have disagreed forcefully while still enjoying a wicked game of bridge. Then—and surely this happened in a wink—my children were the age he was when he died, and older, and he seemed scarcely more than a boy, high-spirited, hopeful, clowning with my pretty mother on a California beach, scribbling earnest endearments to her in tropical heat, and my heart now breaks grieving the death of this beloved child.

# *I Enter Orphanhood*

━━━◆━◆━━━

IN the summer of 1998, my mother's health began to decline precipitously. She'd had a troublesome cough, which she kept saying she "must have looked at," and she began to complain of fatigue. But in May my stepfather had fallen out behind the oleanders and broken his hip in four places, necessitating two surgeries and prolonged rehabilitation. In addition to playing golf and bridge regularly and keeping a social calendar so full that I once gave her a T-shirt printed "Out to Lunch," she now visited him every day and assumed the financial reins he had, as a banker, always held so lightly. No wonder, we thought, she felt worn out.

There really wasn't anyone to look at her cough anyway. The young doctor she'd liked so well had washed his hands of the contemporary medical scene and gone off to grow lemons. And really, who could blame him, since shortly thereafter the owners of the large clinic at which he'd practiced, having pocketed millions, left its gutted carcass floating belly-up. By the time she'd selected another doctor and been given an appointment for September 15, her appetite had fallen off and she felt short of breath. Although the doctor ordered a chest X ray and later a CT scan, then referred her to a pulmonologist — each procedure delayed by the HMO's demand for a utilization review — he indicated no alarm.

As a result, I felt concerned and sympathetic but not alarmed myself until our family gathered at my sister Sally's home near Mother and Dad's in the retirement community of Green Valley, south of Tucson, to celebrate Mother's seventy-ninth birthday at the end of September, some weeks after I'd last seen her. She sat in the same chair the whole time, sipping little puffs of air between outbursts that even codeine-laced cough medicine couldn't calm. She opened her gifts, clearly struggling to show some enthusiasm, though she seemed genuinely excited by the latest P. D. James novel I'd bought her. (The sight of this gift some weeks later, lying untouched on the top of the bookcase, pierced my heart; only death could have come between my mother and Inspector Dalgliesh.) She struggled to swallow a bit of her favorite chicken salad and a few bites of the cake George had baked her. She was nothing like herself: not the young mother who, newly widowed, brought her two little girls halfway around the world and settled them into an all-but-idyllic childhood; nor the middle-aged mother who turned into a whiz-bang town tax collector with a sign on her office wall reading, "Welcome to the friendliest place in town"; nor the retired mother bounding around England, enraptured like me at having our literary studies spring to life. There hadn't yet been time for an elderly mother, who might have been something like the woman sitting beside me now.

I didn't want to leave her that day. I wanted to go to her every day thereafter, but of course I couldn't and would have been of no earthly use to her anyway. That's my bitter reality: I dwell in a body too feeble to take care even of itself. Mother lived twenty-five miles away; I hadn't driven in almost a decade; inter-city buses, eight years after passage of the Americans with Disabilities Act, were still not wheelchair-accessible. Even if I could have made the trip, once there I couldn't so much as pour her a glass of water. She kept assuring me that my supportive calls and notes were enough, and I don't doubt that they were enough for her. Just not for me.

George and I made plans to take lunch to her and my stepfather, recently released from the nursing home, on October 11. The night before, Sally called to report that Mother had fallen and Dad, still scarcely able to prop himself on his walker, had telephoned for Sally in a panic. She would spend the night with them and remain until we arrived the next noon. At my suggestion Sally called the HMO's urgent-care line but was told she appeared to have everything under control. Well, of course she appeared to have everything under control! The mother of a severely disabled daughter, she had spent more than a quarter of a century taking charge of one disastrous situation after another.

"This is beyond us now," I said to Sally as I unloaded myself from our van. "We have to convince urgent care that someone knowledgeable has to look at Mother right now. Have hysterics if necessary. If you can't have hysterics, put me on the line. I'm good at hysterics."

"But Mother doesn't want to go to the hospital."

"I don't care what she wants anymore." Sally had always deferred to Mother more readily than I. "I'll take the blame. I'll tell her it was my decision. We simply can't take proper care of her without knowing what's going on." Later, I would regret this insistence, believing that death might have taken Mother more swiftly at home; and Sally would generously reassure me that, however quick, it could never have been so calm and comfortable as it turned out to be.

No hysterics were required. Sally spoke quietly but insistently, and soon an ambulance was dispatched. I went into the bedroom to tell Mother. A little bag of bones under the bedclothes turned over and looked at me, shaking her head at the mention of an ambulance but offering no other protest. I think she was relieved when the burly paramedics laid her on their stretcher and wheeled her out through a door she would never reenter. We certainly didn't know so at the time. Did she? What does a dying person intuit of the project on which her body has embarked? And if she knew she was leaving home for the last time, did she care? Looking back, I think that my mother had sensed the gravity of her condition, at least for some weeks, and that "home" no longer meant very much to her. She had set out before the ambulance, and she gave no thought to return.

Sally rushed off to meet Mother at the emergency room while we stayed behind to pick with Dad at a lunch he couldn't have much liked (after all, we'd chosen foods to tempt Mother's palate, not his, which was, I suspect he'd have liked to say, the story of his life) and none of us had any appetite for. Not until long after we'd gone home did Sally call to report that the doctors had diagnosed pneumonia, ordered antibiotics, and admitted Mother to St. Mary's Hospital. When we visited her there the next afternoon, we found her sitting up in bed, chatting with the pulmonologist, and expressing an interest in food. The X ray showed a mass, Dr. Coker said, and he planned to do a biopsy in the morning.

"Bye, Mother," I said when we were ready to leave. "I love you." What did she reply? Did she tell me—uncharacteristically—that she loved me too? I wish I could remember, because that was the last time I would hear her voice, that *basso continuo* of my being since sixteen weeks into my gestation.

Our lives were so structured that it made sense for the Green Valley contingent to visit in the morning and the Tucson contingent in the evening, updating each other by telephone. Sally rang me after the biopsy to report that she'd found Mother in the intensive care unit, ashen and gasping behind an oxygen mask; she was so exhausted by the effort of breathing that her attendants soon decided to intubate her, just temporarily, they said, until she was stronger.

"She looks pretty awful," Sally said to me. "Be prepared." But who can prepare for the end of the world as she knows it?

In the evening we found Mother enmeshed like spider's prey in a dim, doorless cell, her wrists tied to the bed rails to prevent her from tearing at the tube that snaked into her mouth and down her throat, her chest heaving in synchrony with the ventilator's *whoosh, whoosh*. Threading my wheelchair past tables and stands and loops of tubing, I pulled up as close to the bed as I could.

"Mother, do you remember telling me about the time I went into hysterics because I was afraid you'd do something bad and the police would come and take you away?" Her eyes half-opened at my voice, and she nodded. My chin resting on the bar that held her in bed, I wasn't much taller now than I had been at that time. "Well, that hysterical child is alive and well inside me. I don't want you to leave me!" She seemed to smile, but I wasn't at all sure she actually knew I was there.

She would never appear any worse than this, it turned out. As a precaution against panic at being intubated, she'd been

sedated with Versed, a drug with anti-anxiety and amnesiac
effects, so that even if she knew we were there at the time, she
wouldn't recall our visit the next morning, when the nurses
cut back on the medication as they began to realize that she
wasn't about to yank out her tube. With the ventilator she was
free of the ghastly choking sensation that had plagued her in
recent weeks, and in the next days she steadfastly resisted all
efforts to wean her from it in preparation for returning home.
Home was not where she was headed.

I wasn't there on Thursday when the doctors told her, but so
closely and constantly did we keep in touch that I feel as
though I was. First they told Sally, Dad, and my half-sister
Barbara, who had flown down from California: the biopsy
showed lung cancer, specifically adenocarcinoma, very aggressive and advanced. She had maybe a few weeks to live.
Then they all trooped into Mother's cubicle to break the
news, somewhat abridged, to her. The family wept, but she
did not. I don't recall ever seeing her cry, though sometimes
she wiped her eyes after hearty laughter. "It's okay, yes," she
penned, unable to speak because of the tube. "I'm seventy-
nine and I'm ready."

    That night, having given a reading at a local bookstore
where I bought a small stuffed Pooh, I took the little creature
to her room. In one of my most contented memories, I am
curled up in bed in my worn Nitey-Nites, leaning into her soft
side, Sally on the other side sucking her thumb—but not me,
no, I gave up sucking my thumb on my third birthday—while
Mother's voice rumbles out Pooh's words, squeals Piglet's,
brays Eeyore's, until the whole of the Hundred-Acre Wood

comes alive in my head. "I want to stay with you every min-
ute and I can't," I told her, "so I've brought Pooh to take my
place. Later, I'll give him to Colin"—her first great-grand-
child. Later, I didn't have to say, after her death.

Because writing cost her great effort, she tried mouthing
her words, which, distorted by the tube, I found all but impossible to interpret, but I quickly caught her question: "How
long?"

"Oh, didn't they talk about that?" I felt a stab of annoy-
ance that the doctors hadn't stepped up to the task, but then I
understood the wisdom of waiting for her to ask what she
wanted to know. It was just my bad luck that she wanted an
answer on my watch. "I didn't talk to them myself, but I got
the feeling from Sally that it wouldn't be long. No, not long."
She appeared composed. Even if she could have spoken, I
don't suppose she'd have told me her feelings. Direct commu-
nication about anything but the weather, which in Arizona
seldom merits comment, was never her style. But, oh, what I'd
have given to hear her voice, even if it only asked me whether
our unusually warm autumn had yet begun to cool off.

"I love you," I continued to say at the end of each visit, and
sometimes now she mouthed "I love you" in return. I didn't
require her response. Although I'd often enough felt that she
didn't like me very much, not always at times I didn't like myself, I never once doubted that she loved me, even though pro-
fessions of affection, beyond kisses at greeting and parting,
would have been dismissed as "gushing." I couldn't now
reach her face for a kiss, so I kissed her hand or her bare toes
through the opening in the anti-embolism stockings they
forced her to wear over her silent but vehement protest. "You

have always been my model of strength," I said at one of these moments. I was serious. To have lived—and lived well—for fifty-one years beyond the death of the man she adored had taken discipline and grace, and whenever I drifted toward self-pity, these were the qualities I sought for myself. But she waved my words aside. Maybe she didn't believe me. Maybe I said them too late. I recalled that when my daughter Anne and her family moved to Denver a few months before, though my heart broke, I also felt faintly relieved of the relentless duty to live up to her expectations, at which I was forever failing. I was worn out from worry that I was at any moment performing the Next Bad Thing. Perhaps I had worn Mother out with a similar severity so that she dismissed her own importance in my life.

Again on my watch, an oncologist came in and offered her some mild chemotherapy. She had stayed with us to help out during several of George's treatments for cancer, so she knew just how rugged chemotherapy could be. We had talked about it several times since, agreeing that in our circumstances we'd refuse it, and she hadn't changed her mind. "I'm dubious about chemo, which seems to be the only option," she'd written soon after her diagnosis. But Dr. Gonzales could offer something unlikely to make her sick. It wouldn't make her well either, of course, but it might shrink the cancer enough to ease her breathing, possibly enable her to stop using the ventilator and go to a hospice facility or even home.

I never heard her express any desire to go home. Sally may have a point in speculating that the idea of being cooped up in the house playing nursemaid to a someone who had turned, in the space of a few months, from a life partner into a crotchety old man so revolted her that she crumpled in the face of it. None of us harbored any illusions about this marriage that had dragged on for more than forty years, though we each had a somewhat different take on it. I viewed it as the desperate act of a thirty-five-year-old widow who might never again have the chance to live a socially normal life. When Mother discovered the magnitude of her mistake, she persisted in it to protect her children from the stench of scandal that, with her parents' divorce, had choked her childhood. By remaining married, she was the object of no one's pity or scorn. She held a respectable place in the town where I grew up; moved to a retirement community in the enviable position of having a healthy spouse; had a companion for her travels; joined the country club and took up golf. A shy woman, she might not have undertaken these activities without the status marriage conferred. But I think her life was bearable only if she and her husband could get out of the house and away from each other regularly. Those days appeared to be at an end.

Going home, then, might offer no inducement to try chemotherapy, but breathing did. "I need to *breathe* before anything else," she wrote.

"Would you consider trying a little chemo if it didn't make you sick?" I asked. Her eyes widened and she nodded. So in dripped the chemicals, which didn't make her sick but didn't have any other discernible effect either.

Anne flew down from Denver for a few days with fourteen-month-old Colin. As Mother's first grandchild, named for her and very like her in her even temperament, Anne had always brought special delight. It seemed a mark of Mother's decline that now neither Colin nor Anne's new pregnancy held her attention for more than a couple of minutes. Her world had contracted to the white island of her bed. Her chief concerns had become the whereabouts of the suction wand that kept her from gagging on her own secretions and whether she'd be given Tylenol-3 to help her sleep.

"What if I want to stop?" Mother turned to me and mouthed one night.

"What if you want to stop?" I repeated. My lip-reading skills were improving, but I didn't want to misinterpret this question. She nodded. "Mother, you're in charge here," I said, grateful that even though she had long had a living will, she remained lucid and capable of making her own hard choices. "You say the word, and we'll set things in motion."

"I just don't want to suffocate," she said. "I don't want to choke to death."

"From what Peter has told me, I feel sure you don't have to," I reassured her. As a pulmonary specialist who works with quadriplegics, my son-in-law's father has turned off a number of his patients' ventilators at their request, and he has assured me that, properly medicated, they die without distress. Because he is one of the tenderest men I know, I would not doubt his word. "She won't suffer, but she might not die right away," Peter warned when I telephoned him that night. "It can sometimes take hours, even days, and it can be pretty awful to watch." I thought we could bear almost anything as long as she was comfortable.

"But it's a Catholic hospital," Sally said when I told her that Mother had mentioned ending all medical intervention. "They won't let her do that, will they?" This is a fairly com-

mon misperception, I've found: that because the Church op-
poses abortion, suicide, and euthanasia, which aim at ending
life, it therefore demands that life be prolonged at all cost (and
preferably with as much suffering as possible). Thanks to irrational practices such as banning the burial of suicides in consecrated ground and persecuting midwives as witches, not
to mention a long-standing reverence for martyrdom, the
bloodier the better, the Church has rather fostered than al-
layed this confusion. But the truth is that no one is required to
take extraordinary measures to remain alive, and the withdrawal of these is permitted, as Father Jim assured Sally when
he stopped to chat with us in the corridor one afternoon.

He'd spoken because he recognized me from that noon's
mass, but I'd heard of him already from Mother, who reported
that he came by every morning. "Do you want me to call him
off?" I asked, knowing that any hint of religion-peddling absolutely fried her, but she shook her head. Apparently, Father
Jim's was just one more disagreeable but necessary visitation,
right up there with inhalation therapy and bed-changing. All
the same, I thought I'd drop a hint.

"My husband and I are converts." I laughed. "But the rest
of the family puts up with our Catholicism pretty well."

"Some of us even admire you for it," Sally said, startling
me. Our conversion had brought anything but joy to our families, especially mine, who had been fleeing the Papists since
before they stepped onto the stark and rocky shore of their
new home in 1620. I'd grown so accustomed to having my
faith politely ignored like a public fart that the thought that
my sister might not merely tolerate but even respect it surprised me with joy. I couldn't imagine Mother, whose hostil-

ity had grown to encompass all forms of religious practice, numbering herself among my admirers, however. If Father Jim caught my suggestion that Mother was not a believer, he disregarded it, continuing to visit her right up until the last morning, when he and I said the Lord's Prayer together and Mother silently joined us, or not, as God only knows.

Several days passed with no further mention from Mother of "stopping." Anne returned to Denver, and after deciding that I needed to spend more time with Mother, I had George drop me off on his way to school and retrieve me on his return. Having persuaded Marla, the ICU nurse, that I could sit quietly and not wear Mother out, I settled in with the text for the medical ethics class I was auditing and made my way through essay after essay on—such are the ironies life permits that fiction does not—physician-assisted suicide while Mother half-watched daytime television and dozed intermittently. I was out of the room, though, when the pulmonologist came by and Mother told him, the nurse reported on my return, "I'm ready."

"Make sure that's what she said," Marla instructed me, so I rolled up close to her bed.

"I hear you're ready," I said, and she nodded. "Are you sure?" She nodded again.

"I'm not going to get better."

"No, you're not going to get better." We had this exchange several times over the days, and each time I wondered whether she hoped for some more reassuring response, but I could tell her only what we both knew. "If you're ready, we need to make some plans." I would have imagined as eerie any scene in which my mother and I—who had collaborated on weddings and anniversary parties, showers and christenings, countless Thanksgiving, Christmas, and birthday celebrations, and two trips to England—sat thus orchestrating her death. Instead, it seemed perfectly calm and natural, the two of us companionably contemplating arrangements for one final major event. It was a Monday; her widowed sister and sister-in-law would arrive the next afternoon; Wednesday was the soonest practical date, and the soonest was what she wanted. In the end, we settled on Wednesday morning at 11:00.

She had never been a patient woman. She regularly drove me nuts by saying she'd come at a certain hour, arriving a half hour beforehand, and then criticizing me for not being ready. "If you'd come when you were supposed to," I'd say through clenched teeth, "I'd *be* ready . . . ," but it never did any good. Now her impatience led to a scene that left me poised between giggles and sobs. A little before 7:00 on Tuesday evening the telephone rang.

"Nancy, I need you to talk to your mother." Marla's drill-sergeant composure sounded a little ruffled. "She won't believe me that it's not Wednesday morning, and she's determined that we're turning off the ventilator *tonight*." Since Mother was enclosed in a cubicle with only artificial light, which blinked on and off at unpredictable intervals, and without a calendar, her eagerness to get on with her appointed task had overridden her sense of time. "She's really quite agitated. See if you can calm her down."

"Oh dear," I said. "I'll try." Although I'd talked with her on the telephone at least once a week since she moved to Arizona eighteen years before, this wasn't going to be one of those long, newsy conversations. This wasn't going to be a conversation at all. Instead of her characteristic deep "Mmmnnnhello?" I heard only the whoosh and suck of the ventilator. My mother had turned into Darth Vader. You can't die yet, I had to tell her, it's too soon, it's still Tuesday, Barb and Joe haven't arrived from California, you have to wait twelve more hours and do it as we planned. What on earth must she have thought as I rattled on earnestly? For me, that was the hardest part of those last mute days: that I couldn't ask her what was on her mind. She probably wouldn't have told me much. Although she talked a great deal, she almost never confided intimate thoughts or feelings. I didn't care. The voice that had filled my ears since gestation was stilled, and I was without solace. "Now put Marla back on," I said.

I had complained more than once of finding Mother so heavily sedated that she couldn't be roused, but now I asked the nurse to give her some Versed to get her through the night. When I got in early the next morning, she seemed alert and fairly calm. She kept an eye on the clock, though, and by 10:00, when the family still hadn't showed up to make their goodbyes, she was decidedly restless. How exasperating to have one's very death delayed by family disorganization! Then they arrived and went in, two by two, to say goodbye. By God, at 11:00 sharp her four children and husband gathered in her room and Marla turned on the drip of morphine and Versed.

When Marla came back fifteen minutes later, Mother roused and mouthed, "I don't need this," pointing at the blood-pressure cuff that had been irritating her for more than two weeks and smiling at her own joke.

"No, I guess you don't," Marla said, removing it. Mother turned her head and closed her eyes for the last time.

At 11:30, Marla turned off the ventilator and wheeled it out of the room, which was suddenly quiet. A few minutes later, noticing that Mother was moving her legs uneasily, she increased the flow of medication. "It must have been something, having her for a mother," she whispered on her way out, and we all smiled in affirmation. It hadn't always been easy having someone so bright, opinionated, and directive at the heart of our lives—but it had always been *something*.

The next time Marla came in, I asked, "How's she doing?"

"Well, she's dying. At this point, mostly from the drugs." She looked straight at us. "Is that all right?" We nodded in unison and resumed our vigil. Mother's face paled steadily. The monitor faced us. Each time Mother's heart rate dropped to a lower decade, I cheered her silently: "Atta girl, Mother, you can do it!" It dropped below thirty, then down to zero, up again, down, and the line went flat. It was 12:20. "I've done a lot of these," Marla would say to me when I left the room, "and I've never seen anything like this. I've never seen anyone die so fast." "You didn't know Mother," I'd reply. "She *said* she was ready."

For a few moments after the monitor squealed, we sat silently, gazing at the still form—paper-pale skin, gaping cyanic lips—that had been Mother and now suddenly, inexplicably, was not. Mother was gone. I had never seen the process of death straight through before, and I understood now why people find it deeply mysterious. Mother was there—wasted and sedated, to be sure, but recognizably herself—and then she wasn't. Who, then, was "she," and where had she gone? The conventions of my faith claim that she was an immortal soul flown up to heaven, but these are concepts even I can believe in only figuratively, and they would doubtless seem even more far-fetched to my secular stepfather and siblings. Yet before our eyes the body had discernibly altered. Something—call it spirit, anima, vital spark, life force, what you will—had departed.

And with its departure, we were no longer held by the bedside. Almost in unison, we sighed deeply, broke into smiles, and reached for one another. The joy that bubbled in me radiated from the others' eyes, whether teary or dry. As Sally would say at the memorial service, her death was Mother's last, best gift to us, a final instruction in responding to all life's exigencies with dignity. Rather more clumsily than Mother might have approved, we trooped through the ICU to the waiting room to embrace her sister and her brother's wife, her sons-in-law, two of her granddaughters—all our family events have been large and noisy.

I was, as usual, wearing a hat, a soft tan crocheted cloche, which was, as usual, too large for me. Pulling away from the others, Aunt Jean bent down and said, "When you were little, you pulled your hat down around your face like that, and your mother said, 'Don't do that, you look like an orphan.'" What we looked like never having overly concerned either Jean or me, we laughed at this motherism. "And now you are one!"

And now I was one and would remain, whatever else I became, for the rest of my days. At the instant following Mother's final breath, the abyss of abandonment on the brink of which I had teetered, terrified, since I was four yawned and swallowed; immured there, with no father, no mother, I was henceforth wholly on my own.

After Granna, my mother's mother, died, I remember yearning to offer Mother some adequate expression of sympathy, but I never found it. My muteness embarrassed me, but only now do I begin to understand that it signified not some character flaw or failure of love but simple ignorance. I couldn't think of words to comfort Mother because I had had Mother to speak them to. I had thus found her loss utterly unfathomable. In the months following Mother's death, I would experience it myself and find others—my children not among them—with whom I shared it. I felt then as though I'd entered some new terrain, hitherto unsuspected but not therefore uncharted. I've had this experience time and again, most dramatically when my husband was diagnosed with stage-IV melanoma, almost invariably fatal. It occurred to me then that, although I had entered the world of the dying, plenty of people were ignorant of such a place, in just the way I had been before his diagnosis. One world had not replaced the other; they existed synchronously; only I had been dumped unceremoniously out of one into the other. Now I found myself displaced again, joining those who are no longer anybody's children.

"I miss my mother!" I burst out suddenly one evening more than a year later. The intensity in my voice startled me. And the friend to whom I spoke, whose own mother has been dead for some years now, responded with the Irish lilt that thirty-odd years have not eradicated (her mother's voice, no doubt), "Oh, I know. Not a day goes by . . ." She still thinks of her mother every day. She will always think of her mother every day. As will I. As I have done all my life. Death seems unlikely to break such a habit of mind. We all know our mothers for at least the months of gestation, and some studies suggest that even those who are separated from their mothers at birth may harbor a subliminal sense of loss. Those of us who, for better or worse, have sustained enduring relationships with our mothers—whether biological or adoptive—surely do not lose the sense of connection when our mothers die, though it may take on a grievous tone, at least for a time.

What I have lost is the foremost figure to stand between me and death. As long as the generation before us remains intact, we can persuade ourselves that it's not our turn: the old ones must go first. For me that protective wall began to be breached unusually early, with my father's death; and in recent years the rifts have become more numerous, frequent, and severe. Now my vulnerability feels complete. As does my adulthood. I am the old one. I defer death for my children. "I wish I could come with you, wherever you're going," I said to Mother the night before she died. She frowned and shook her head, partly to deny that I should have reasons for wishing for a hasty death, I'm sure, but also perhaps to remind me that it *wasn't* quite my turn. She was always making me wait for something: lipstick, nylon stockings, a black dress, my first sweet milky cup of coffee, my first cocktail. Now I've got to wait to die. As an orphan, I have work to do.

# Aftermath

SALLY refused to schlep Mother across the country in her carry-on bag. She began to dither: the weight would be too great to sling into an overhead compartment; the urn would shatter, strewing Mother every which way (though she was well constrained in a heavy-duty plastic bag). "Good Lord, I'd take her," I said, "but I've got to go to Dayton for a few days first, and I don't think Mother *wants* to go to Dayton." Although we'd held a memorial service right after she died eight months ago for her Arizona friends, Mother's ashes were to be interred beside her mother's grave in Massachusetts, we always knew; and at last all four children could make the trip at the same time.

In the end, Sally wrapped Mother in layer after layer of bubble wrap, Styrofoam, and cardboard and shipped the enormous parcel to her mother-in-law, who lives just outside Boston. This arrangement seemed acceptable, since Mother and Zelda always got on well; and Zelda had the good sense, when her daughter, visiting from Israel, inquired about the box in her closet, to say, "Better you don't ask."

Thus, by the time we all converged, Mother had already been waiting for us for some days. On a hot afternoon in late June, she sat primly by the gray granite headstone engraved "PEDRICK    CUTLER" at the top of the Wenham Cemetery, and one could all but feel the tap of her toe as two o'clock approached, arrived, and then washed past in a susurrant flood of greetings and embraces. One might think we didn't know any better. But of course we knew better. Look who reared us. We were simply caught up in the delight of looking into long-loved faces, some of whom we hadn't seen in years, some of whom, in view of their ages, we likely would not see again. Even Sally didn't seem pressed to begin, though Sally is the one of us children who has become Mother. ("It's official," reads the mug Sally's daughters gave her a few years ago, "I have become my mother.")

Finally—and really only about fifteen minutes behind schedule—we turned our attention to the minister for a simple burial service. As I listened to her soft, clear voice, my eyes swept the slopes outside the cemetery wall where bright golf carts sped from hole to hole. That's where we should be, I thought. Mother had no patience with prayers, but she did enjoy a round of golf. *What on earth are you doing here?* Mother herself would ask, her voice edged with exasperation. *On a day this hot, why don't you all just go to the beach?*

We were certainly not standing around murmuring the Twenty-third Psalm for her sake. She had precious little use for mumbo jumbo. Oh, she was a regular churchgoer when I was young, but in the 1950s in a New England village that was how you marked your social place: not among the Episcopalian estate owners or the superstitious Catholic immigrants, both groups having to leave town to attend services, or the Bible-thumping Baptists on the outskirts, but with the solid citizens of the First Church in Wenham, Congregational, at one end of the common, opposite the post office and the town hall, square in the center. A young widow without acquaintances, as Mother was when we moved to

Wenham, could ill afford to leave her position and allegiances undefined.

When, in the 1960s, such conventions began to crumble, her attendance at church grew sporadic and then ceased altogether. By this time she had remarried, and since my stepfather was town treasurer, their social position was clear. He was no churchgoer, though, having had a horrific religious upbringing; their children, sent to Sunday school unaccompanied by either parent, stopped going as soon as they were permitted. In recent years Mother and Dad played golf on Sunday mornings. God is present on the links as everywhere else, I'm sure, but Mother would have dismissed such a notion with faint hostility. God had long since fallen from her good graces. Indeed, I am the anomaly in my family: neither parents nor siblings nor children have active religious lives. We were hardly here, then, as I might be among my Catholic friends, to pray for the repose of Mother's soul.

Each of us children spoke briefly and then, at the minister's invitation, some of the others offered reminiscences. My eyes stung with sweat, not with tears. I — who used to vex Mother with my everlasting emotional gusts — have not wept over her death, or anything else, for many years. Squinting against the light, I floated in a bath of memory. This cemetery was not a spot I spent much time in. From here, a small group of us trudged out onto the golf course, often through snow, for a sunrise service every Easter. And of course I marched here, wearing my Girl Scout uniform, in the town parade on Memorial Day. Mother was never along on these occasions. The only time we stood here together was nearly thirty years ago on the January day, gray and unseasonably mild, when we buried her mother. The ground had been soft enough for a grave to be opened, and we stood at the raw verges as the casket was lowered before trooping down the hill to the church (Granna having insisted that her body not be present at the service), where we sang "I Come to the Garden Alone," and then on to Aunt Weez and Uncle Dick's for a tumultuous family gathering where Granna was present as she had always been, only in whichever room one was not, my first adult experience of the psychological "undeadness" of the dead.

Granna had prepared us thoroughly for this event. Having been told four years earlier that she had an abdominal aneurysm, for which there was no treatment in those days, she had had ample time to contemplate her death, and since, like most of us, she preferred companionship in her deliberations, it had been the topic of conversation at the dinner table more than once. Although these scenes might seem the stuff of some Southern Gothic novel, in our Yankee household they were neither lugubrious nor macabre but purely practical, right down to the favorite hymn, so that when the time came, no one should be at a loss. Having served on the planning committee for Thanksgiving, Christmas, every graduation and birthday party, wedding, baptism, and funeral for as long as any of us could remember, subsequently serving as a chief celebrant, Granna was bound to "live" for us at her own farewell.

This consolatory consciousness of the beloved as present though elsewhere has remained with me since that day. I feel Mother with me always, just out of my line of sight. Like an infant who finally grasps object permanence—the fact that a toy or a person exists even if unseen—I can carry the idea of

Mother in my head. It's a different stage of cognitive development, however, in that whereas the infant learns that the mother, though absent, will always return, I must content myself that the mother who will never return remains with(in) me nevertheless. Sometimes I can't. On the night of the last episode of "Inspector Morse" on PBS's *Mystery!*, I simply wanted to ring her up and commiserate on the loss of our favorite detective, over whom we'd sighed like schoolgirls for years, in conventional Alexander Graham Bell fashion, two audible voices in each other's ears. For the most part I am just grateful that death has proved powerless to snatch her away. I feel her alive in me, in my DNA, of course, and in the biochemical storms of memory.

Our relationship was at its most passionate during the years when we lived together at the edge of this village of fewer than three thousand inhabitants north of Boston, where she and Granna, a widow and a divorcée pooling their modest resources, bought half an acre of land and built a little Cape Cod house. How they conceived the scheme and settled on the location I don't know. Damn! Another uncertainty I can't resolve. This is a grief I never anticipated: that my sources have died, taking with them the answers to all kinds of questions I never knew I would ask. The two women chose well, at any rate. Wenham was then, and remains today, strikingly pretty, from its sweep of lake at one end through its maple-lined main street of colonial houses out to the acres of open and wooded land that have so far escaped the clutches of greedy developers. Moody and romantic, I ranged over this area on foot or bicycle in all seasons and weathers, shuddering with ecstasy. A childhood spent in a state of bedazzlement like this creates a lifelong habit of looking and loving, and I've always been grateful that Mother plunked me down in surroundings that biased my being toward beauty.

My life here was sheltered in a way that is hard to imagine today. Although I knew enough not to accept rides from strangers—Granna warned me of being "killed, or worse"—Wenham was so safe that I could amble or pedal along country roads without a stranger ever offering me a lift, let alone attempting murder or that mysterious "worse." There was no racial tension for the simple reason that there was only one "race." The poorest people in town, though they had bad teeth and beat-up cars, lived in houses and had food on their tables. Burglary and vandalism were so rare that I can't recall an instance of either. Everybody knew not just who everybody else's children were but what they were up to, and they were all happy to broadcast their observations. I found this vigilance claustrophobic and invasive; I resented it; yet I counted without question on being cared about by all the world as I knew it. What I did mattered: to teachers and the school-bus driver, to the minister and congregation at church, to the town librarian and the postal clerk. And although these strictures resulted in a parochialism and naïveté that retarded the development of my social consciousness, they didn't inhibit it altogether.

At the center of this snuggery was Mother, to whom I was attached with the focused ferocity of the child whose father vanishes before she can distinguish death from abandonment. If one parent could slip away between bedtime and breakfast, I reasoned, so could the other if I didn't keep careful track. Early on, I never took my mental eyes off her, and gradually I fell into the habit of relating every element in my world to

Mother. Not that I always deferred to her judgment or behaved in ways guaranteed to please her, because as I grew
older I assuredly did not, but that in my choices great and
small—of clothing, of reading matter, of men to date, of subjects to study, of political causes to pursue, of spiritual practice—I remained attuned to the likelihood of her approval or
disapproval. Though unaware when I was young that I believed my mother to be a deeply unhappy woman, I continually worried that I was in one way or another either failing to
moderate or outright adding to her grief.

That this fixation upon Mother's well-being might be in-
terpreted as odd and even unwholesome didn't occur to me
until, at nineteen, I was preparing to get married. A couple of
college friends who were going to be my attendants accompanied Mother and me in the search for a gown. Although I
leaned toward one cut close to the body and appliquéd with
lace and pearls, I chose the less sophisticated (and less expensive) one, plain and full-skirted, which Mother said suited me
better. That night when my friends found me huddled in a
chair in the dark, sobbing because I was going to be married
in a dress I didn't much like, they couldn't understand why I
didn't just tell Mother I wanted the other dress instead. I
didn't know how to explain that having been married twice in
blue suits, Mother needed the wedding of her dreams, and
mine was going to be it. When my own daughter informed me
emphatically that she intended to have her wedding just as she
wanted it without any interference from an overbearing
mother thank-you-very-much, I was amused. Having relin-
quished a wedding of my own, I was more than willing to let
her have hers.

Although over time and with no small pain I carved out a self that was not my mother, I remained vulnerable to her anger well into my thirties. And I continued to consider my actions in terms of her response long after that response ceased to shape them. Just a few years ago, having commissioned a local muralist to paint an enormous and elaborate Virgen de Guadalupe on my studio wall, as George and I contemplated the outcome I burst out laughing: "Oh Lord, what is Mother going to make of this!" It wasn't any longer a real question, since Mother's reactions could be predicted pretty reliably, but an acknowledgment of her presence in my affairs. Even today, when she is no longer around, I gauge the events of my life partly through Mother's eyes. Perhaps all daughters do. My father's death may have tinged my attachment to Mother bright with an anxiety not all children may feel; but the primacy of that attachment strikes me as merely human.

Although Mother's personality was strong enough that everyone at her graveside must have viewed her with at least some of the ambivalence my memories reveal, the voices around me recalled only sterling qualities, of course. This was a funerary rite, at which the speeches are, by long custom, eulogies. We may remember the dear departed's darker attributes well enough in our private moments, but in public we must only praise. I could understand, even approve, the convention: this was, by design, a celebratory occasion. Whoever heard of a "dyslogy," and anyway that's not what I had in mind. I just wished someone would recount an anecdote that portrayed the complicated woman Mother was.

Like our conversation in the garden in Kent, England.

With Mother and Dad, George and I rented a cottage there for two weeks in July 1994. Bouncing along in her Reeboks like a schoolgirl, Mother made a delightful traveling companion, and day after day of glorious weather had put us all in a mellow mood. But this day, as we sat on the terrace amid the clematis, stock, and roses sipping our drinks before dinner, she somehow got onto the subject of a beloved nephew's divorce, for which fault had to be found. In Mother's world, innocence could never belong to more than one person at a time.

"I'm not surprised he didn't stay married to Tess," she said. "I never could warm to that woman." Thus was Tess judged and dismissed, not for the first time. I hated the meanness of spirit Mother's pronouncements too often betrayed, and I knew that if she made this one to me, others in the family had heard it, too. She was making a fool of herself, and I was letting her.

"Tess isn't to blame for the divorce, Mother," I said. "James is gay."

Utter silence. I swear the bees stopped droning in mid-flight. The baby birds in the nest behind the foliage ceased screeching for their large speckled mother and shut their maws. My heart halted between thuds, appalled. Never having talked with James about his coming out, I had no right to announce his homosexuality to anyone, and I felt ashamed even as I knew I had done what I had to do.

"Oh," said Mother at last in her low voice. "Then of course Tess isn't to blame for the divorce. And neither is James. Nobody is."

I could have hugged her, except of course that I'd have betrayed my surprise and relief at her response, hurting her feelings. A woman of strong opinions, with a clear sense of exactly how life ought to be lived, she had scant tolerance—and that grudging—for those who deviated from her views and practices. That these were social rather than religious in character made them no less hidebound. Yet suddenly, at the age of seventy-five, drinking vodka and tonic in an English country garden, she had struggled with her certainties and leaped beyond them into pure emotional generosity. When we returned home, she wrote James a loving letter. And she firmly told an uncle who complained that he could no longer count himself a Unitarian now that homos were being ordained that she didn't permit gay people to be disparaged in her home.

I saw her grow in similar ways throughout my life, the hide of self-certainty—toughened by Puritan tradition, social propriety, and educational convention into a singularly parochial moral vision—suddenly split and peeled back to reveal a tenderer creature within. For a variety of reasons—chief among them, I think, my father's death—she could not allow herself to live thus exposed, and soon she was bound by new hide, but each time larger, looser. Watching her small metamorphoses, I learned that adulthood was not a state to be achieved but a process to be refined. This is the mother I'd have liked to reveal at her memorial but couldn't in such a setting. I came as close as I decently could by reading a poem I wrote twenty-five years ago that ends:

> Mother, it is so peaceful here, with you,
> Now that I am going away.

The reminiscences trailed off. Clutching my hand as tightly as she used to do when she was a toddler, my half-sister Barbara sang the Lord's Prayer. Her voice—which, though not professionally trained, is low and strong and sweet—scarcely quavered despite her tears. My half-brother, Nathan, lowered the brightly painted Mexican jar holding Mother's ashes into the square hole dug for it. Clasping hands, the assembly formed a large, irregular circle for a last blessing. As they dispersed, I peered into the hole and called down softly: "Goodbye, Mother!"

There must be funeral meats, of course. Mourning and eating have been intimately linked since Paleolithic times, when food offerings were placed in Neanderthal graves. The pre-Columbian Mexicas, providing sustenance for the journey of the dead through nine underground passages to one of three final resting places, bequeathed customs that became, when filtered through Roman Catholicism, Mexico's Día de Los Muertos, with its gay graveside picnics complete with bone-bedecked bread and crunchy sugar skulls. Other groups throughout the ages have sought to take on the powers of their dead or simply to honor them by ingesting them—not their representations, confectionary or otherwise, but parts of their actual bodies—sometimes to their grave detriment. Until quite recently, the women and children of the eastern highlands in Papua New Guinea suffered from a rare and fatal neurological disease called kuru ("shaking" in the Fore language), which resulted from the custom of consuming the brains of the deceased.

Today in New England we neither feed nor eat the dear departed, but we do regale their mourners. No riotous Irish wake for us Congregationalists, no meal of condolence or protracted Shiva, but at least a token of hospitality. I suppose that the provision of refreshments, whether simple or lavish, at ceremonial gatherings has practical roots in the days when people might spend some time traveling, by slow and arduous means, to pay their respects. They might well need to eat and rest before retracing their route. The social obligation to make a cordial gesture tends to outlast—or perhaps merely exceed—any recuperative need, however. I remember how the custom irritated my daughter when, while she was a Peace Corps worker in Zaire (now Congo), the adult son of one of the local farmers died. Even the most distantly related family members gathered at Tata Nzulu's home and remained until the last crumb and drop had been consumed. Even then, some mourners continued to ask for more. Through hard work, Tata Nzulu had achieved relative prosperity, to which my daughter had hoped to contribute by teaching him how to breed fish for food, and she resented the way the occasion of his deep grief served to drain his resources. That tends to be the way of customs, though: the need to observe them may have little to do with their practical impact.

Often the provision of postritual refreshments is made easier by the custom of taking food to the home of the bereaved, on the well-founded premise that, in the turmoil, they will have little time or appetite for preparing proper meals. To be sure, such offerings may not include the Double Gloucester-shire layered with Stilton and Kendall-Jackson chardonnay that my friend Mary brought me following Mother's death, but even a tuna casserole can come in handy. After the first funeral and burial I ever attended, that of my paternal grand-mother when I was fifteen, I recall the solace of gathering at the home in Kennebunkport, Maine, where so many of us spent at least part of our summers for a supper of ham and baked beans and apple pie. To draw together for a meal both nourishes the mourners, affirming life, and encourages the flow of reminiscences that keeps the departed one present in our midst.

But today we have no vast Kennebunkport kitchen in which to assemble a repast, no home here at all. We've all left Wenham, and the only family members in residence here are the ones in this cemetery plot. Still, we wanted to spend a little more time with those who had come to remember Mother, some of whom I, the longest gone, hadn't seen for at least a quarter of a century. We asked the ladies of the church to set out some punch and cookies in the Parish Hall and invited everyone to join us. There, I caught up with the lives of children I used to baby-sit and their nearly grown children from mothers whose faces, though broadened and creased and wreathed with silver hair, remained familiar. I wondered whether they were searching past the lines and gray, past the wheelchair that propels my twisted form, to descry the girl who romped with their infants forty years ago.

Assaulted by the heat and the conversational din, I was pretty well wrung out by the time the last of the mourners had left and we loaded my wheelchair into our rented van.

"Let's go to the water," I said to George, longing for the only natural solace my chosen desert existence denies me. We drove up Main Street, by the brick post office and fire station, still yellow clapboard and gray shingle in my mind, and the white colonial where we lived the year after Mother and Dad got married. Turning at Dr. Boothby's house, we followed the narrow, looping length of Larch Row, past Roddy Ar-

cher's and Maddy Woolf's and Sarah Norton's, through the
Four Corners with the Sterlings' gray hulk on one side and
across from it the square house where brilliant, strange Laura
Kane lived until she vanished into Radcliffe, up the incline
where Uncle Sid's house and barn stood until they burned
down, and so—just before the town line where Larch Row
becomes Essex Street—to 236, the modest cape where I did
the most critical and excruciating of my growing up. Once set
rawly at the top of an open slope, planted round with foot-
high spruce and pine seedlings, it is now nestled so deep in ev-
ergreens as to be nearly invisible.

Because I never learned to drive while I was living at home,
Mother drove me along this route hundreds—no, thou-
sands—of times. Now whenever I ride along it, I feel the
queer doubling of vision, of person, that comes when I physi-
cally revisit sites from my past to which I usually return only
in memory. I have no idea who lives in any of these houses
now. It is as though each of them is peopled simultaneously by
strangers and by my remembered friends—long lost, gone
who knows where. In the same way, the house in front of
which we briefly parked, whatever the welter of unknown
lives it now contains, also shelters the ghosts of the woman
who built it and occupied it for almost thirty years and of
those of us who shared it with her for various intervals during
that span. As they twist the doorknobs to our rooms and polish Mother's cigarette smoke from the windowpanes and stow
stray items in the odd little closet in the stairwell where
Granna used to keep her hats, do they sense our shades drift-
ing among them?

I'm not asking whether they hold séances where my siblings and I tip tables, our childish voices screeching forth from the mouths of entranced strangers. As far as I'm concerned, the only things that go bump in the night are of human, canine, or feline origin and altogether of this world. All the same, I think of places as inspirited somehow—perhaps at the subatomic level, each of us trailing a veil of quarks that mingle with those in our surroundings—by all the creatures who once inhabited them. This fancy may explain why I have never yearned, as so many Americans do, to build my brand-new "dream house." That house, in holding only my own dreams, would seem a sterile space. Despite the narrow pipes and blown fuses and squeaky floorboards (though I've never had a wall fall off as my aunt and uncle did in their colonial farmhouse), I've always sought out older houses. Not that I have anything against "mod cons," which I add in as I can afford them. I just like knowing that others have lived their own mysterious lives here before me. Or died, for that matter. George and I bought our first property, a graceless Massachusetts duplex, from the estate of a sizable man who had slumped against the bathroom door, giving those who found him a devil of a time getting at the corpse. I hated that house, but I also hated the city in which it was located and the life I lived in it. That was simply my reality then. "Bad vibes" (as we would have called them in those days) from a death in the bathroom had nothing to do with my loathing, though asbestos shingles and leaky faucets surely did.

In the top right-hand corner of the battered bulletin board by the back door of our current house in Tucson is stapled a pen-and-ink sketch of a barn owl. It's there not because I know the artist, which I don't, or because I think it's an undiscovered masterpiece, which it isn't, but because it was there when we moved into the house fourteen springs ago and no one ever got around to taking it down. Now I'm inclined to leave it there, concrete evidence that this space has sheltered prior lives, including the life of an anonymous artist who probably did not go on to become the new John James Audubon. One of the consequences of the modern western habit of constructing the cosmos in relation to the personal self is that we too readily believe that entities spring into being for our use, exist as long as we need them, and vanish at our departure. The owl reminds me that my house is indifferent to my occupancy, having harbored one tenant after another for sixty-five years. If the greedy maw of the neighboring university weren't to devour it and spew out an asphalt parking lot in its place, as is likely to happen before very long, it could go on performing its task indefinitely, the ghosts of tenants past thronging—young selves and old selves alike—thicker and thicker until the atmosphere would seem, to the sensitive, to shimmer and sigh.

All this is pure fancy, I must add hastily and a little defensively. Some readers insist on taking one at one's word, and I dread the spreading of the rumor that Nancy Mairs has gone right round the bend and thinks she lives in a haunted house. I'm simply inventing a figure that conveys the ineffable sense I have, gazing at my childhood home, both that the cosmos transcends our brief incarnation in it and that, at the quantum level, we are in it and of it forever. I've never glimpsed a ghost (except on occasion, out of the tail of my eye, the shadow of one beloved black cat or another) and don't expect to do so. I was beside Mother when she died and have seen the little that was left of her interred. She is gone for good. But if, as Heinz R. Pagels proposes in *The Cosmic Code: Quantum Physics as the Language of Nature,* the breath I just took in contained an atom exhaled by Julius Caesar when he groaned, "Et tu, Brute," why not a mote of Mother? And nothing short of my own death can eradicate her from my every cell.

Pulling away from the past-ridden house, we wound out to Route 128 and, at its end, on to Gloucester, where townspeople and tourists, celebrating St. Peter's Fiesta, with the annual blessing of the now sadly depleted fishing fleet, washed the dingy city in color and sound. Bobbing along in my mind, Mother tutted, never having had any use for such primitive peasant rituals, though she was happy enough walloping a little dimpled ball with an iron rod. But George and I enjoyed strolling along the waterfront to watch the contortions of some young fishermen competing to walk along a heavily greased pole suspended from a platform high above the water and then a rowing race. The Gloucester restaurants were overflowing with revelers, so we drove on out to Rockport and meandered Bearskin Neck until we found a place that could accommodate us. In my mind Mother seemed to feel more at home here, gazing out at the fishing shack so commonly depicted that it has come to be known as Motif #1 and munching on a lobster roll.

Weary, we returned to our motel, trailing Mother and the rest of our dead ones like a perpetual imperceptible mist. When we were very young, George and I concur, this seemed the smallest of clouds, not much bigger than the balloon Winnie-the-Pooh used to disguise himself from the honeybees, and we seldom thought about it. With the passing years, it has grown bit by bit and the pace has picked up, especially since we joined our support group, Living with Cancer. We are still far from the point that the majority of our friends and relations have died, but we've already known quite a few elderly people in that position.

One of them, our beloved friend Elizabeth McKinstry, reached the age of ninety-five. Elizabeth was what might be called (though never by Elizabeth) a "pistol": smart, outspoken, given to exuberant gestures (fueled in part by an exuberant love of whiskey neat) and admirable aplomb. As she flung her arms wide to greet her company one evening—so the story goes—one of her breasts leapt forth from her décolletage; popping it back inside like a naughty puppy, she carried on without a stammer. How I wish I'd known her in those days. Or even earlier, when she picked up her husband-to-be as they stood between the cars on a train headed for Albuquerque. Because he died of cancer before they were fifty and we didn't meet her until she was in her seventies, we never knew Hugh. And yet we did, in the way one comes to know the beloved dead of those one comes latterly to love. Not all the ghosts who populate one's life are one's own.

A mineralogist at Harvard, Hugh traveled a great deal throughout the world, and because they had no children ("the great tragedy of my life," Elizabeth once told me), she accompanied him. After he died, she kept up with their far-flung circle of friends and continued to ramble. She must have been nearly eighty when, deciding that the Pacific was the only region she hadn't sufficiently explored, she booked passage on a freighter bound for Micronesia. After that she stuck more and more closely to home and, in her final year, remained in bed, sedated by morphine, with round-the-clock attendants to see to her scant needs. The only person to visit her frequently was her longtime friend Bev, who saw to her affairs. Stopping by early on the day Elizabeth died, Bev found her quite animated. "Oh!" Elizabeth had said. "So many friends have been in to visit that I'm quite worn out." No, the attendant said as Bev left, no one had come. That night, Elizabeth drifted away forever.

So common are visitations in reports of near-death experiences (NDEs) that I, for one, do not expect to die alone. Once again, I dread the eye-rollers and scoffers who will label me a naïf if not an outright nut. And I can't altogether blame them, since accounts of these experiences can make for some mighty strange (and not overly literate) reading, filled as they are with buoyancy and tunnels and light and spirit guides that may include telepathic pets. When NDEs are put forth as evidence of an afterlife, then I side with the skeptics, because the narrators have uniformly returned and dwell in the now, not the sweet hereafter. But when the skeptics (altogether too often characterizing themselves as scientists) go so far as to claim that NDEs don't "really" occur but are "only" caused by brain chemistry, then I grow impatient. What the devil do they think "reality" is if not the product of cerebration? "Reality is merely an illusion," Albert Einstein pointed out, "albeit a very persistent one." I may assume that "reality" exists apart from my own or anybody else's consciousness of it, but that's all I can do: make a rough hypothesis. There's no "out there" out there that "I" can know; and if, after my death, there turns out to be, "I" will no longer care. Meantime, I give myself permission to imagine that my dear dead ones will come for me. Their point of origin—angelic realm or dying brain—matters not at all.

Not long after the death of Rosemary, another dear elderly friend, one of the founding members of the Community of Christ of the Desert to which George and I belong, the group devoted an evening to remembering her. George, who is one of the quieter participants, had been sitting with his eyes closed, smiling, as we recalled details: Rosemary's passion for both horse racing and opera; the naturalness with which she moved among convicts, the homeless, refugees, homosexual men, and what passes for "high society" in Tucson; her deep devotion to the woman she always referred to as Our Blessed Mother. As our reminiscences trailed away, George sat up and said, "I have been looking at Rosemary as God sees her, and God takes no notice whether she is dead or alive. That distinction has no meaning for God. And it doesn't have to for me, either." He couldn't sustain this cosmic vision for long. Who among us—except a saint or a mystic—could? But his insight has stayed with me.

This is the miraculous message of the resurrection, it seems to me. Not that a body nailed to a cross died, was entombed, disappeared, and was later seen and spoken to by grief-stricken friends more than once before rising like a hot-air balloon through the clouds and vanishing into the Garden Spot of the universe with the promise that, if we were good enough, we'd get to go there too. Even though I have elected to believe this story, as most of the world does not, I don't think it details what is going to happen to us when we die. I think it as much analogical as anagogical: a rough suggestion, in terms the human imagination can conceive, of our permanence in the cosmic Working Out we know as God. Because our selves are all (with which) we know, our visions are bounded by their realities: we will fall into a sort of sleep and then wake up, arise, put on garments of light and a pair of wings, pick up our harps, and break into song, behaving, in short, rather as we do now only better. The continuity, in recognizable form, of ourselves and those we love, because it can't be disproved, can hardly be condemned. I'm just not counting on it.

The wonder indicated by the Christian resurrection story —and by other tales, whether religious or secular, which attempt to point toward realities that are humanly unknowable —is that death does not from some perspectives occur at all. The fact that we believe in it as an absolute end says more about our limitations than it does about either the event itself or the universe in which we are embedded. Because it is, without question, the absolute end of the personal consciousness beyond which noesis no longer functions, we require faith (though not necessarily religious faith) to proceed any further; and faith, as the (doubting) Thomas of the resurrection story demonstrates, comes hard to some of us—and to others, not at all. Faith requires a kind of letting go—a relinquishment of any pretense of control and an admission of radical ignorance—which, in the name of intellectual rigor, modern thinkers tend to resist to the (excuse the expression) death.

"Seeing is believing," most of us say along with Thomas, as though human vision were some arbiter of reality, although our eyes perceive only a fraction of the spectrum. Few of us doubt, however, that on either side of the rainbow's red and

violet lie the infrared and ultraviolet. What is it but faith that
leads us to pop some frigid yummy into a large box and press
a few numbers, confident that within minutes we'll be sitting
down to a passable imitation of a hot meal? I've long since
learned that when my Labrador retriever's ears prick, George
will shortly pull into the yard, even though my own ears can't
yet detect the rumble of the van's motor several blocks away.
And I don't question the physicists' observation that my dense
and sullen body is made up, at the atomic level, almost entirely of space or that the flutter of swallowtails across my
yard may trigger a torrential downpour in Madagascar. "If I
have told you earthly things and you do not believe, how can
you believe if I tell you heavenly things?" Jesus asked his
followers (John 3:12). A more apposite question nowadays
might be: If you are so credulous about earthly matters, some
of them really quite far-fetched, why should the idea of tran-
scendence so try your faith?

I don't know what has become of my mother. This ne-
science I must accept—embrace—as part of what defines me
as a human creature. I know that Mother is humanly dead. I
sat beside her as she died. I handled her ashes. I saw these put
into the ground. Yet she certainly lives on in the memories of
many. Her genetic legacy (and her mother's, and her mother's
mother's . . . ) abides in her scions. And if matter and energy
are indeed conserved as scientists assert, then she has not been
destroyed but translated into an existence no less authentic for
my inability to read it. On the myriad occasions when I long
to speak with her, this conviction provides cold comfort. But
I'll take comfort at any temperature I can get it.

# Regret, Revision, Release

ALTHOUGH at the moment my mother died I became, in the strict sense, an orphan—both my biological parents were dead and I had not been adopted—I was not entirely without a parent for a few more months. Mother had remarried seven years after my father's death, and so I had had a stepfather for forty-five years. With Mother he had two children "of his own," but he treated us all evenhandedly. His name was Nathan Hayward Cutler, but I called him Daddy. (Although I have always distinguished between my two Daddies readily enough, others might confuse them, so I refer to my stepfather in this book, as I have never done in life, as Dad.) During my typically tempestuous adolescence, we had our share of shouting matches, as parents and children do, but there were quiet moments, too, like the time when, a hurricane having knocked our power out, we sat in lantern light side by side at the piano while he helped me learn the Bach Prelude in C. He never said a lot to me—or anyone—directly. As a bank manager and town treasurer, he occupied a prominent position in our community, though, which put him in touch with a lot of people, and every so often someone would report that he'd been boasting of my accomplishments. Over the years, he took me to my first baseball game, attended the performances and ceremonies in which I appeared, came to Fathers' Weekends at college, "gave" me to George in marriage, held my babies gingerly, loaned George and me money for the down payment on our first house: all the acts whereby a man in our society lays claim to a girl as a daughter.

Dad's life ended pretty much the way you hear about nowadays. Except for a case of chicken pox brought home by his children, his adult years were plagued by little more than the common cold. Blue Cross–Blue Shield must have loved him. Then, in the final year or so, great energy and expense were required to keep him going. In the backyard trimming the oleanders, he fell and broke his left hip in four places, necessitating two surgeries and months in a rehabilitation facility. Without even rudimentary knowledge of the structure and functions of the human body, he was the worst patient imaginable, wholly demented by anesthesia and morphine, truculent and easily confused even when they were out of his system, uncooperative with his therapists, unwilling to adapt to his changed condition. Almost as soon as he returned home, his wife sped off in an ambulance and, just more than two weeks later, died. Now he was on his own with no idea how to take care of his most basic needs and no inclination to learn.

Living only a few blocks away, Sally bore the chief burden of Dad's care. A home health-care worker came in for two hours every day to straighten up the house, make his peanut butter and jelly sandwich for lunch and a dinner he could heat up later in the microwave, and do his laundry. But the squamous cell cancer removed from his scalp some months before had now metastasized to the underlying skull, and Sally drove him five days a week for seven weeks for radiation therapy. Twice daily, she also changed the dressing that covered the wound, which was open down to the meninges, enduring his shouted curses when she hurt him, as she was bound to do. She drove him to the dentist when he broke a tooth, to the medical supply store when he needed a new walker, to the shoe store and then the clinic when he needed a lift on his left shoe.

Sometimes I feared his behavior would drive Sally beyond even her formidable powers of endurance. He was plainly relieved that Mother was gone and made no effort to hide his contentment. "I want to shout at him," she'd confess, " 'Damn it, my mother is dead!' " He developed a passionate attachment, more infantile than erotic, for his home health-care worker, a lively woman about our age who cut his meat into tiny bites and rubbed lotion into his back and feet. He re-fused to consider moving into an assisted-living facility; he rejected a LifeLine for emergencies; then he telephoned Sally (or sometimes, addled, Barbara in California) for help. Be-tween his intermittent confusion and his deafness, he had trouble understanding what people said to him and snarled at them over the telephone or in public, mortifying Sally. Like a small boy, he reported his bowel movements, mortifying her in private as well. Refusing all exercise, he spent his days shuffling financial papers at the kitchen table, though Mother had given him a handsome roll-top desk, or lying in his re-cliner watching ESPN and reading the sports page.

I was restricted to my usual cripple's role, euphemistically described as "moral support," and I wasn't always good at it. One day Sally reported that his recliner had begun to smell pissy from numerous little accidents he had when he failed to wake from one of his frequent naps in time to get to the bath-room. "Take some of my chair pads," I instructed, long since familiar with every incontinence product ever devised, "and tell him he has to put one under him wherever he sits so he won't ruin the furniture."

"I can't do that!" she wailed. And she was right. Though a genius at dealing quickly and practically with both major emergencies and daily trivia, she isn't comfortable with confrontation in potentially embarrassing situations.

"Of course you can't!" I said warmly. "And I shouldn't have asked you to. But here's something I can do. I'll take care of it." And I wrote down some suggestions for preventing and managing incontinence and sent them straight off to him.

Sally was the one called when Dad failed to open the door for his worker, the one who found him unable to speak clearly or get out of bed, and the one who rang the ambulance for his last trip to St. Mary's. He appeared to have had a mild stroke, as we suspected he had had the week before when he fell and spent a long and miserable night on the floor; the doctor admitted him for tests. We left him in good spirits, enjoying his supper of sirloin tips, relaxed about the next day's procedures, joking about his forgetfulness. "I'm a nincompoop!" he said as we headed for the door.

"You may be many things, Daddy," I called back to him, "but you're no nincompoop. I love you!" And I rolled on through the door and down the corridor.

We were waked the next morning by the telephone. The doctor had called Sally the previous night to report that Dad had had a seizure and had been taken to the ICU for observation, but he was alert and seemed all right. When she got to the ICU for the 8:30 A.M. visit, however, she found him semicomatose, and by the time George and I got there, he couldn't be roused at all. The staff wanted to know immediately whether they should intubate him. Remembering Mother's wretched days on a ventilator, we thought not. Unable to reach Barbara and Nathan for concurrence, but knowing

Dad's wishes from his living will, we asked that he be kept comfortable but not otherwise treated, and they began to give him morphine. He looked dreadful. He'd recently had a deep-tissue graft to his head wound, and the hospital doctors, terrified of infection (and with good reason, because there's no buggier place), had ordered a huge bandage. White gauze wrapped around his head and under his chin gave him the appearance of an elderly nun. Without his partial plate, his face appeared sunken. Once the oxygen mask digging into his face had been removed, however, he appeared at ease.

Exhausted, Sally headed back to Green Valley for the water exercise she needs in managing a ruptured disk, and George went home to take a shower. "I just sit anyway," I said. "I might as well sit here." So I bought a detective novel in the hospital gift shop and parked my chair within reach of Dad's hand, still elegant in old age, with long, slender fingers and shapely nails. I didn't know whether he could feel my touch, and I was sure that without his hearing aids he couldn't hear my murmurs, but perhaps in some other way he could sense my presence. Anyway, these gestures comforted me. "I love you, Daddy," I said every so often, sometimes aloud, sometimes not. "Go gentle."

A flurry of voices outside the room began to talk to someone named Marla. I went to the door and, sure enough, there stood the nurse who had attended Mother's death. Catching sight of me, she hurried over. "What are you doing here?" she asked.

"Now Dad's going."

"Oh, Lord." She rolled her eyes. "You're getting to be quite an expert at this, aren't you?" I nodded ruefully. I had never envisioned myself engaged in a death watch. Most of us don't when we are young, I think, both because we're kept away from the scene by the solicitude of our elders and because, although at some point we learn that we too will die, that moment still seems impossibly far away. A good many deaths occurred in my family as I was growing up, but the process always played out elsewhere. If I ever saw the person again (as I did my grandmother Garm), the event itself had already taken place, the embalmer had plied his trade, the product was finished in every sense of the word, all without regard to me.

The first dead creatures I ever handled were the various kitties and puppies, bunnies and guinea pigs and mice, even a checkered garter snake that we wrapped in household linens and buried in the backyard as our children grew up. These interments were the occasion of copious tears and occasional hilarity, as when George finally had his father's doddering beagle Vicky put down. He brought her home, put her in a pillowcase, and laid her on the porch while he dug a hole.

"Don't bury her just yet," I said, "because Anne's coming by shortly, and she might like to say goodbye. After all, she's known Vicky most of her life." Soon my daughter Anne and now husband Eric arrived. Since they'd only recently returned from their Peace Corps experience in Zaire (now Congo), and we didn't yet know Eric very well, I was uncertain how he'd react to a dead dog on the porch awaiting Anne.

"What," he said when I explained that we were about to bury Vicky, "without freezing her first?" At my puzzled look, he explained that while he was in Zaire, his family's elderly cat had died. In Denver in midwinter they couldn't bury her, so they stuck her in the freezer until the ground thawed.

"Eric," I laughed, "I've been worried that this family

would be too weird for you, but I'm not going to worry any more!" How a family takes care of their dead pets can tell you a lot about the openness and affection with which they view the rest of creation. I knew I could love people who cleared a space for Kitty among the chuck roasts and packages of peas on the middle shelf.

When George developed metastatic melanoma a decade ago, my world shifted suddenly and sharply as I took up residence among people who were dying. To everyone's astonishment but his own, George himself did not die, but a good many people in our Living with Cancer support group did, and then family members and close friends in the generation before ours began to go, too. I'd never been present at the event itself until Mother's death, but I'd long since grown comfortable in the presence of the dying. This ease, I suppose, was part of the "expertise" to which Marla referred.

Before long, Dad's breathing became stertorous. I began glancing at the monitor. His heart rate, which had been strong and steady, now began to fluctuate more and more widely. His skin paled. I recognized the signs, and I was startled. I had assumed we'd be given more time, enough for George and Sally to return to the hospital, maybe enough for Barbara and Nathan to make the trip from San Francisco. No one had suggested that he would go so soon. He took a last raling breath, and then the room was silent. I have never felt more alone. I wanted Mother, dead nine months before in a bed just a couple of rooms away from this one. But Mother was doubtless glad—if anything of the dead survives to feel gladness—to be well away from the whole experience. What mourning was to be done fell to his children.

* * *

I think Dad loved the four of us insofar as he was capable of love, but the truth is that, emotionally speaking, he was something of a basket case. His father had died before Mother and Dad met, and I know of him only that he had a sweet singing voice and that a bout of polio had forced him to give up working on the family farm. Dad's mother was a truly chilling woman, squat and sour-faced, who boasted that until he was four she'd confined him and his toys to a playpen. On Sundays, while the neighborhood children ran about like rowdies, her children Nathan and Marjorie had sat properly on the front porch and watched. Perhaps not surprisingly, Marjorie had her first nervous breakdown at fifteen and matured into a querulous (and, following the miscarriage of twins, childless) woman capable of abiding interest only in her body's largely imaginary ills and ails. She continues, even in the grip of Alzheimer's disease, to wage war against dust mites and acid reflux. Lack of maternal affection and the absence of playfulness were compounded in Dad's case when a mastoidectomy to combat an infection following measles caused a loss of hearing that deepened over time.

As a result, although escaping Marjorie's neurasthenia, Dad grew into a reserved and rather solemn adult, forbearing but capable of startling outbursts of real meanness when his patience was overtried. Because no one ever identified him as disabled—not even I until many years into my own disability—and addressed his difficulty in interacting with others, his social skills remained limited. As soon as Dad graduated from high school at sixteen and went to work as a bank messenger, his father quit his job delivering milk and Dad became his parents' sole support—a situation unconducive to marriage, though he must have had some hope since the engagement ring he gave Mother was not newly purchased. By taking night courses in business and banking, he was able to improve his position to the managerial level. He appeared to like his work and to be good at it, but he never displayed fervor for it or any other pursuit, even his beloved golf.

He and Mother met late in the summer of 1954 at the home of mutual friends who planned an evening of bridge for that express purpose; they were engaged a month later and married on October 23. Why on earth did they do it? At the time, teetering on the verge of adolescence and steeped in sentimental fiction, I assumed that they loved each other, that being the only reason I'd ever been given for marriage. Forty-five years later, almost to the day, I can see that although I had to relinquish any romantic notion of their relationship fairly early on, I continued to assume that they *liked* each other, at least a little, not because they actually did (I have grave doubts now) but because I needed to believe that they did. The thought of their staying together without any affection was too painful to explore, and it suited me to have them together. In a life wrenched by my father's death, which remained for me emotionally chaotic for a very long time afterward, this partnership served as a constant. Since Mother's death I have been racked by guilt that I abandoned her to her loveless life. I suppose this is a common element in grieving: regret—arrived at always too late—for having failed to be the perfect daughter (spouse, sibling, friend) whose vigilance and sympathy would have soothed the slightest pain.

Anyway, I have no idea why Mother married my stepfather, and I never asked her. Last night a friend told me that her very elderly mother has begun to recount stories from her marriage, and I groaned with regret for all the stories I will never know because I failed to ask and listen before death cut them off. I don't suppose I'd ask Mother about this matter even if she were still alive, though, lest I be suspected of questioning her judgment. But the truth is that I do now question her judgment, and his as well. Except for the fact that they both played good bridge, they knew scarcely anything about each other. Aside from good looks and respectability, they had little in common. She was the hybrid scion of old Salem and Marblehead stock and a German immigrant butcher's family, reared in comfort, well educated, and more than a little snobbish; he, solidly working class, lacked the polish she valued. She read literature; he, sporting news. In restaurants she ate seafood, preferably shellfish; he, only steak. More to the point, he had never lived with anyone except his parents and was most likely (or at least as good as) a virgin. She had been married for almost six years to her heart's desire, a handsome and brilliant naval officer, from whose death she had not recovered in seven years—and would not recover in forty-four more.

I suppose they ran out of patience, not that either of them was cynical enough to recognize such a motivation. But at thirty-five and forty-one, she and he had both endured years of eligibility in a society that absolutely could not tolerate anything unmatched—socks, purses and shoes, candlesticks and the candles in them, people. An unpartnered man or woman was, well, odd; and a suitable mate must be scouted out at once. Dad must have endured his share of "introductions" (adults didn't get "fixed up" or go on "blind dates") as did Mother, I know firsthand. She had at least one serious suitor, the wealthy son of a family friend, whom she spurned because he didn't like children and would have packed us off to boarding school straightaway, Sally and I were told. Thus were we reassured of our superior value in Mother's eyes, though I must confess to an occasional ignoble wish, when I grew sick of second-hand clothes and cars and furniture for which "patina" was a mere euphemism for "scratched, gouged, faded, and frayed," that she had gone for the money.

What better way to silence the indefatigable matchmakers than to give them what they wanted? And if the match were not exactly made in heaven, well, which of them had purported to be an angel? I can't tell anyone born after 1950 just how relentless was the message that *any* marriage was preferable to staying single. And a childless marriage was almost as pitiable as none at all. So of course Mother and Dad had children, and the bunch of us became every television-watcher's American family, minus the laugh track. If anything was wrong with the picture, I certainly did not know it; I attributed any uneasiness I felt to my own weird nature, which didn't seem capable of sustaining happiness for more than a few manic hours at a time. Also, I lived in this family for fewer years than the other children—six, compared with Sally's nine and Nathan and Barbara's eighteen—and so I may have a more limited and idealized view of its dynamics.

During the last two decades of Mother and Dad's lives, I spent more time with them than did any of the others, because they retired to Arizona while Sally remained most of that time in Massachusetts and the younger siblings moved to California. I spoke with Mother on the telephone at least once a week, and we got together for all holidays and birthdays and often for no particular reason but affection and an evening of bridge. We talked about a wide range of issues, events, and people, but never in depth. Twice George and I traveled to England with Mother and Dad for two-week holidays, and although we irked the living daylights out of one another at odd intervals, as weary travelers are wont to do, our foursome proved surprisingly companionable.

They seemed content enough with their lives. They enjoyed separate activities—Dad was an Elk, and Mother belonged to the American Association of University Women—but they also watched sports programs and played golf together. They had more money than they had expected to have in retirement, with which they bought and maintained a pleasant house, joined a country club, ate out several times a week by themselves or with friends, traveled to New England every summer to visit family and old friends, even threw themselves a fortieth-anniversary party (figuring they might not live to the fiftieth, as indeed they didn't). That this was merely the occasion for throwing a bash rather than the celebration of an enduring relationship went without saying.

Why, having made the error of marrying in the first place, had they compounded it by staying together? Barbara recalls that, at the time she divorced her first husband, Dad spoke of wishing he'd had her "chance," and Mother must have longed for another life as well. But, for better or worse, they were a little too old to join the lemming-rush of couples to the divorce courts which mirrored the rush to the altar of earlier generations. And once Nathan and Barbara had been born, the matter would have been especially fraught for Mother, whose parents had divorced amid some public nastiness when she was eleven. In a community as small as the one I grew up in, I don't think she could have faced the scandal. For the sake of the children, in order to save face: theirs was hardly the first marriage to have been held together by such glue.

Then, too, in those days one required grounds for a divorce, and what grounds would they have given? Certainly not their dismal sex life, at which they only hinted while their separate beds shouted it aloud. Nor adultery, though Mother must have been tempted after her high-school sweetheart reentered her life in 1958. She told me once though that she'd always resisted and, all too sadly, I believed her. God knows the "irreconcilable differences" cited in most divorce cases of the day would have been true enough, but the failure implicit in that phrase would have rankled. For these two Yankees, lying—even with gritted teeth—in (twin) beds of one's own making would have seemed the more honorable choice. In the end only death would part them.

One effect of their dying, which I hadn't anticipated, has been the freedom to look squarely at their lives. But another is that I've lost the sources who could verify or repudiate my interpretation. I may have got it all wrong. The past is ripe for falsification. Since my father-in-law's death, for example, Mum Mairs attests that "in our fifty-one years of marriage, Bill and I never had a cross word," though George can remember from childhood his father's shouts and his mother's tears, and I, having known them since I was seventeen, heard my share of exasperated snaps and sighs. But she has chosen to recall a relationship blander than a nursery pudding. What if I've done the same in reverse, remembering only Dad's churlishness and Mother's furious needling? They may not have cared much for each other, but they made a tolerable life for themselves and their children. Why shouldn't that be enough?

It has to be. The injunction not to speak ill of the dead has its practical as well as its superstitious basis. That is, even if they won't come back to haunt you (and chances are they won't no matter what wickedness you utter), neither can they confirm or deny whatever you say. They are, quite literally, beyond reproach—or any other sort of declaration—and without question. No longer verifiable, all your statements, however true you may believe them, become after death a form of fiction; and you, the author of the past, may tell the story as you will. Most of us, if we are sane, do so in the very best of faith, striving to remember and represent what "really" happened. Because the past exists nowhere but in our minds, its "reality" is always only a construct—and one that shifts depending upon who we are and what we need at any given time. To speak—thus remembering—ill of the dead illuminates not their lives but our own.

At the end of my parents' lives, they were not happy, and I see now that, in my grieving, I have viewed the whole of their lives through the lens of the end. To take such a view is characteristic of my mental style but not of theirs. Once, when I told Mother that I'd read a piece by a disabled person who characterized himself as "constitutionally cheerful," she commented, "Well, I am, you know." As a clinical depressive, having the opposite constitution, I couldn't imagine what such cheerfulness might feel like, but I believed her. I have not falsified the details of her mismatched marriage, but I have certainly misrepresented her experience of them. Call it repression, call it denial, call it defense mechanism, but the truth is that over the years she exhibited considerable enthusiasm for her life. And despite his acute reticence, Dad did, too, especially after retirement when he twice hit a hole in one and won the member–guest tournament at the country club.

"Leave the dead to bury their own dead but as for you, go and proclaim the kingdom of God," says the Jesus of the Gospels (Luke 9:60), and his injunction is less severe than it might appear at first glance. In context, it reminds would-be followers of the paramount importance of serving God. But, as with all the best passages of the Gospels, it speaks to non-Christians as well in a resonant call to life. He does not suggest forgetting or otherwise dishonoring the dead; rather, he calls us to relinquish them and get on with our work.

One of the tasks falling to us children was to sort through Mother and Dad's personal and household effects, keeping some for ourselves and our children, placing some with a resale shop on consignment, giving the rest to the White Elephant. We might have found the process lugubrious, I suppose, but since levity is more our style, it soon turned into a celebration. In a welter of clothing, linens, furniture, and knickknacks, our voices tumbled over one another: "I'd love to have that if no one else wants it." "Ooh, that's really ugly. Whatever possessed Mother to buy it?" "What on earth *is* that?" (In a couple of cases, we never figured out.) Because many of the articles evoked memories, we soon felt Mother and Dad in our midst. Now in the morning George may tug on a pair of Dad's socks. I may slip Mother's strand of garnets over my head. We light rooms with their lamps and seat guests on their chairs and rub ourselves dry with their towels, keeping our sense of connection.

On my sideboard rest a tea canister decorated by Mother with decoupage, which contains a few of her ashes, and a Mexican tin box with Dad's ashes. Once I might have thought that such keepsakes exhibited the macabre bathos of bad Victorian art, and the startled and dubious expressions of some acquaintances suggest that my nature, rather than the nature of the mementoes, might have changed. Not everybody is put off by them, though. When a friend's mother died, we compared our mothers' ashes (hers were coarser and darker) much as we might once have compared the living women. On a visit not long after Mother's death, Barbara spied the canister and, pulling off the lid, called into it: "Hellooo." I know Mother would have helloed right back if she could. I like these natural and humorous responses, which fit the companionable sense the two little boxes provide me. There they sit, separate yet side by side, rather the way their two occupants lived their lives. Releasing myself from grief and guilt, I simply take comfort from their presence.

# Lost Children

*For Shane Locke Hasbrook, August 19, 1997–July 15, 1998*

"OH, you'll *love* being grandparents!" people exclaimed whenever George and I announced that our daughter, Anne, was pregnant with our first grandchild. "You get to spoil the kids rotten—and then give them back to their parents!" We chuckled politely, but each time we heard the same idea voiced in virtually the same words, our smiles grew more forced. I have no idea who first uttered these words. Perhaps at one time they seemed fresh and funny, but now overuse has reduced them to a social cliché.

I can grasp the appeal of this one. None of us ever liked to discipline or deny our children. Still, children can act in dangerous or offensive ways that require correction if we want them to live into healthy and socially responsible adulthood. Few of us have the financial resources to gratify the proliferating desires a consumerist society churns up in even its youngest members, and we wouldn't have done so anyway, since a surfeited child may be ill prepared to make wise choices or to cope with life's inevitable shortfalls and losses. When I think back to the difficulties of mothering young children, though, fatigue looms larger than discipline and denial, and perhaps this is what my friends' platitude refers to: the relief, so often longed for but impossible to secure as a parent, that comes from knowing that you can go off duty soon.

94

However the phrase is taken, it seems to George and me woefully insufficient to communicate our complicated responses to our new role. For me, these began with a burst of gratitude that, thanks to modern reproductive technology, my beloved daughter would not be deprived of her heart's dearest wish, long deferred by an inexplicable failure to conceive. She bloomed from the beginning, and the baby did, too. We saw the first picture five weeks and a day after conception, and this was followed by videotape at regular intervals. In March, during a backward somersault with legs widespread, he revealed his sex spectacularly, and in May he received his name: Colin James Mairs Peterson. Because my wheelchair put me at just his level, I had been talking to him all along, even before he had developed ears. Now I could address him by name when I babbled the polysyllables his father, Eric, was convinced would increase the neuronal connections in his brain. "Colin," I would murmur. "I love you, Colin. Prestidigitation."

"Silly old thing," my daughter's expression plainly read, but I ignored her. What could she know about becoming a grandmother? On Mother's Day she wrote me a lovely letter, which read in part: "I realize now that no one can really understand the bond a mother feels with her child except another mother. Not even the child, as much as she may love her mother, can understand the love a mother can feel." She hasn't extrapolated this insight to grandmothering, though. How could she? Although I was fortunate in knowing and believing myself loved by a grandfather, both my grandmothers, and three great-grandmothers, I had no inkling that I might occupy more than a peripheral position in their busy grown-up lives. Unlike information, emotional knowledge comes only through experience. Once acquired, however, it can't be lost: within the grandmother live on the mother and the child. This certainty gives aging a sweetness the young can never comprehend.

I sat with Anne throughout her labor. In fact, the next day I couldn't think why my muscles were sore until I recalled that I had made every last push with her. When the obstetrician, having exhausted his bag of tricks, threw up his hands and said, "No way is this baby coming out this route," Anne was crestfallen. "Don't fret, lovey," I said to her before she was trundled off to the operating room. "This isn't a failure, just another way of getting a baby." An hour or so later, I went with George and Eric's parents to the recovery room. Anne was sitting up in bed, the baby clamped to her breast, tears pouring down her pale face, her voice trembling: "He's—so—*beautiful!*" In the sight of the child I once suckled now nursing a child of her own, I glimpsed eternity.

I have always felt myself to have been a bad mother, depressed and snappish and bossy, too quick to scold and slow to praise my children, unable to fathom or meet their needs. George finds my self-condemnation odd, but the other day over lunch a friend said, "You know, the best thing about being a grandmother is that it gives you a second chance, a chance to do right all the stuff you loused up the first time." We both laughed, wondering if there's a woman in the world who believes herself a really good mother. Apparently, guilt is less common among fathers, but then they don't experience the expulsion from the womb, the thin accusatory wail that pierces the maternal heart. *I'm sorry,* the mother's subconscious cries out. *I'm sorry I ejected you from perfect warmth and nourishment into the chancy world.* And goes on crying ever after.

Anyway, I've always believed I made a proper bungle of the job, and this time *I don't have to do it!* I thought with exultation from the start. I could simply let Colin be whoever and however he becomes. One night when we were baby-sitting, he set up a howl. Oh, the piteous pout and tears! When he didn't settle down in half an hour, we bundled him up and set out through the moonlit streets. "You may think you're driving us nuts," George beamed at him complacently through the wails, "but you're a flop. We adore you no matter what you do." When the carriage began jiggling over a brick sidewalk, Colin grew quiet, somber at first and then cheerful; by the time we strolled into our yard, where his parents were waiting, he was chortling aloud. We loved it all.

This equanimity has proved one of the dearest gifts of grandmotherhood. As Colin grew heavier and more wriggly, my arms were too weakened by multiple sclerosis to hold him, but for a few weeks I could put him on a pillow in my lap and dote on him while he slept. As I was engaged in just this rapt activity while a family birthday party roiled around me, my son-in-law approached and asked, "Were you this way with Anne and Matthew?"

"Oh no, nothing like!" I laughed. "Then, I was always anxious, fretting whether I was taking good enough care of them, giving them the right food or clothing or advice." Eric laughs, too. Like me, he's a worrier. "Now all that is up to you and Anne. I feel nothing but pure joy. I'm not sure you can grasp what I'm talking about until, one day, Colin makes you a grandfather. But trust me, it will be worth the wait."

* * *

The blissful few months when Colin lived only a mile or so away ended when, upon Eric's graduation from medical school, the three moved to a Denver suburb, where they've been joined by baby brother Trevor John Mairs Peterson. Although we see them only infrequently, telephone calls, e-mail, videotapes, and snapshots keep us up to date. Trevor can walk now, they report, and he's a dab hand with any kind of ball. As Colin acquires language, he has moved beyond merely pointing out his world's contents—the mail truck, the garbage truck, the concrete mixer, the crane—to fathom its workings.

"Colin, you're being too mean," Eric chided him not long ago.

"I am mean," he replied. "I'm Cruella," the archvillainess of his favorite Disney film.

"If you go on being so mean," Eric warned, "you'll have to have a time-out."

"Cruella doesn't get time-outs." Just so early does a child come at a bit of moral knowledge that will dog his choices the rest of his days: that evil-doers go unpunished just as often as not, no matter what Big Daddy says.

Although I wish I could observe their development firsthand, I find my separation from them natural. Both George and I observed early on that grandchildren have nudged us to one side of the stage that all the world is. For most of our lives we've formed the primary family constellation: father, mother, daughter, son. After Anne and Matthew left home, although this unit no longer existed in fact, nothing else replaced it; and so we continued to consider parenting our chief role. Now a child has herself become a parent, creating a new constellation in which we will, if all goes well, play an ancillary part. (All does not always go well: when I had a nervous breakdown just before my daughter's second birthday, my mother took over Anne's care for several months, though with such tact that Anne never lost track of who and where her mother was.) The world's chief biological and social tasks—the replication of DNA, the reproduction and refinement of mores and values—no longer belong to us. We are now, quite literally, beside the point.

Rather than making me feel old and used up, this insight relieves me, contributing in large measure, I'm sure, to my growing indifference toward death. I've had enough of center stage. I'm tired of mattering. I don't know how people without children develop such detachment, though having observed that they do, I must assume there are manifold other means for learning that the world can get along without one's continual close supervision. I'm simply blessed to have as teachers Colin and Trevor, who have no earthly need for me. I don't at all mean that they'd be better off if I just cleared out. On the contrary, having known my own grandparents, I can attest to their emotional and cognitive value in a child's life. They are the "old ones," whose memories insert us into history by attesting that at one time not only did we not exist (our parents have told us that) but, unimaginably, *our parents did not exist*, thereby rousing us to awareness of a time from which we were wholly absent. And if a past without us exists, why not a future? These first gentle intimations of mortality nudge us toward a grasp of the human condition.

But conveying such lessons requires more a structural than

a personal role. That is, essentially any person of a certain age possessing sufficient tenderness and goodwill can play it. A mother, by contrast, is absolutely particular. Studies and anecdotes suggest that no matter how early and eagerly a surrogate steps in, an infant separated from the birth mother will undergo some degree of trauma. Very quickly, the mother, even if a surrogate, must be *this person and no other,* as any woman knows who has had to pry desperate little arms from around her knee in order to leave her child with a baby-sitter. A grandmother—unless serving as the surrogate mother— can pretty well come and go as she pleases.

While I live, I can hope to enrich the lives of my grandchildren. I certainly don't intend to "spoil them rotten," whatever that unsavory phrase may mean. Love spoils no one. Unable to offer them any physical assistance, I can at least listen to them, admire them, celebrate their being in the world. But if each of us lives out our allotted span, already well over the biblical three score years and ten and lengthening with each new medical discovery, I cannot possibly outlive them. Nor have I any motive for doing so. They will grow up without me. They will grow old. They will die, leaving children and grandchildren who will grow up and old and die. None of them need me—or rather, whatever they might need me for I have provided them already.

Their very presence announces that although I will die (perhaps before they know me and certainly before they know what they mean to me), the human project will continue in ways that I can scarcely dream and probably wouldn't approve if someone asked my opinion. My grandmother Garm disliked my wearing boys' shirts. (And so she bought me a blouse with fishing flies embroidered on it. Go figure.) When my son grew a ten-inch red-and-yellow mohawk, my mother wouldn't let him leave her house for fear her neighbors would see. Since they've been doing so throughout history, I assume the old are supposed to view the young as harbingers of degeneracy. Civilization as we know it has always teetered at the brink of extinction in somebody's eyes (though it's less likely to be pushed over the edge by the harebrained fads of youth than by the terminal fuddy-duddiness of us old ones once medical researchers have figured out how we can stick around indefinitely). At some point, owing to ill humor, profligacy, and/or hubris, the human project may indeed fall apart, leaving the cetacean project or (more likely) the cockroach project in its stead. The sun may engulf the Earth and reduce it to a cinder. Our galaxy may crash into the galaxy next door. The entire universe may collapse upon itself. No matter how curious I am about these scenarios (and I am, very), I needn't worry about them. I am not in charge. "All shall be well," I assure myself in the medieval mystic Julian of Norwich's words, "and all shall be well, and all manner of thing shall be well." In cosmic terms I think she is absolutely right.

In human terms, I am aware that the joy and confidence of such a vision rest on certain premises about the way the world works. In particular, I assume that Colin and Trevor are cherished by their parents, in whose care I may safely leave them, and that they will indeed outlive me, free from injury and in robust health, no matter how long I hang around. It occurs to me that those of us born in the twentieth century are the first human beings who could hold such a blithe belief—and then only if we chance to be born into privilege still undreamed of by most of the world. I recall, on a visit to my daughter in Zaire, sitting in Ma Charlotte's kitchen, a bare area at one side of her little mud-brick house, when we heard a ululation not far off. A young man came up and said to me in schoolboy English, "A child has died." Using my schoolgirl French, from Ma Charlotte I gathered that a three-month-old infant had died two days earlier, probably of malaria. Three men came down the dusty track through the village, the middle one bearing a tiny blue bundle, followed by a group of people, then a mama alone, keening, and another group. The villagers wailed as each passed. At the sight of the little blue bundle and the sound of lamentation, my own eyes filled. Here, Anne had told us, babies are hardly acknowledged during their first year, so uncertain is their survival.

Without access to antibiotics, immunizations, or even sanitary water, they are vulnerable in ways many of us can hardly imagine: malaria, of course, but also encephalitis, AIDS, sickle-cell anemia, parasites, snake bites, infected scratches. In some villages, all children under the age of two have been wiped out by measles. The simplest diarrhea can be deadly. And they starve to death in huge numbers, victims of war, famine, natural disaster, and political expediency. Throughout the world people die of starvation at the rate of one every 3.6 seconds, and three-quarters of them are children under five, according to The Hunger Site. (Visit the Web site www.thehungersite.com once a day, click on a button, and the site's sponsors donate staple food to be distributed by the United Nations World Food Program.) The mind does not easily wrap itself around such numbers, which is why I found my experience in Zaire invaluable: it drove home the fact that every death, everywhere, marks the loss of a specific being and must be mourned accordingly.

Even in the United States, until well into the twentieth century, childhood—like the whole of life—was chancier than it is today. Scarlet fever, diphtheria, typhoid, and tuberculosis were commonplace. My grandmother really did have a friend who died from scratching an insect bite, though I thought she was making the story up to scare me. Before spraying to control mosquitoes became widespread, a friend reared in the South recalls having malaria. Everybody had measles, mumps, chicken pox, and rubella. I'm just old enough to have known a number of people who had polio, sustaining various degrees of damage; many others died. In 1957, when my cousin was born at seven months weighing just over three pounds, his survival was deemed something of a medical marvel; nowadays, he might have made it at half that size. By the time my own children were born in the 1960s, I had every expectation that they would live into adulthood—and such expectations were founded not on wishful thinking but on hard scientific data.

Despite extraordinary leaps in public health, immunization, treatment, and technology during the twentieth century, babies don't come with guarantees, even when they're conceived and born in the most medically advanced parts of the world. From the outset things simply go wrong sometimes. Chromosomes get misplaced, or lost, or doubled. Pregnancies terminate, either spontaneously or through medical intervention. Fetuses get damaged in utero or during birth. All too many infants die of neglect and abuse (even one is "all too many"), but the most conscientious parent can't prevent every illness and accident, and some of these are fatal. Looking back, I'm astonished that my children reached adulthood with no evidence of childish close calls except for a pock mark on the bridge of Anne's nose and a lump of scar tissue on Matthew's forehead where it connected with a golf club during one of his spacier moments. But I don't want to look back in this way. Even in the safety of retrospective imagination, the thought of harm coming to my children makes me squirm.

Who can contemplate the death of a child, their own or anybody else's, even a total stranger's, dispassionately? It appalls in a way no other death can do because it violates the natural order. Never mind that the true nature of nature may be chaotic, falling into patterns that possess great power to disturb. To give life shape and sense, we've created a schema in which a carefree childhood (whoever dreamed up that codswallop for the period most fraught with mystery and menace?) is followed by a vigorous and productive prime, a (recently invented) leisurely ripe retirement, and only then senescence and death. We don't readily tolerate any deviation from the script, especially not one that snatches away a being who represents both prelapsarian bliss and the life of the world to come.

In the days when the children around us were all too likely to die, we tended to distance ourselves from their painful reality by sentimentalizing them: Christmas-cheerful Tiny Tim; Blake's chimney sweeper (almost sure to be dead of scrotal cancer by puberty) crying *weep, weep;* beatific Beth March, whose sisters will grow past little womanhood without her. Even bathos might be preferable, however, to the modern tendency to depict the deaths of the young not in personal terms but as news items in a culture that considers reportage a form of entertainment, as remote from everyday life as the latest Hollywood release. Anonymous images of skeletal figures lying on bare mattresses in hospitals without medicines or clinging, eyes and lips covered with flies, to equally emaciated mothers have been beamed to our television screens from other continents; even the plump childish faces that gaze from newspaper stories of drive-by shootings or backyard drownings come from some other state, or city, or neighborhood, or family. . . .

But what if they don't? What if one of them appears in our midst? What if the grief comes home? Miscarriages, birth defects, and SIDS occur in every locale. Despite enormous improvements in the odds, illnesses like cystic fibrosis and leukemia—even, under certain conditions, appendicitis, food poisoning, and the common cold—can still be fatal. If carelessly attended, children drown in the bath, eat poisonous substances, stick their fingers in electrical sockets, choke on small objects, chase balls into the street. Many are killed in auto accidents, especially if not adequately restrained. Some are shaken or beaten to death. A few are abducted and murdered. Most horrifically, especially in adolescence, our children drug, cut, starve, shoot, or hang themselves. Although overall suicide rates have remained about the same over the past fifty years, according to Centers for Disease Control statistics, the rate for teenagers has nearly tripled.

Despite losses to disease, drunkenness, and despair, however, we will rear most of our children into adulthood. One of the consequences of having them well insulated from most forms of disaster is that we are poorly equipped, individually and as a society, to accommodate it when it occurs. We haven't the practice of an Indian or an Iraqi or a Congolese parent. Not that the loss itself comes more easily to such a parent—some experiences absolutely do not admit comparison—but that denial of the very possibility of loss and consequent grief have not deadened or deflected feeling in response to such loss as it can in us.

This denial begins in earliest days. "Don't cry!" a mother says to her toddler when the string on his bright helium-filled balloon escapes his chubby fist and the treasure bobs off among the treetops, although crying seems the most sensible response to such a loss. She means only to comfort him, of course, and quiet his sobs; but by using the imperative, she has issued a command. "I'll get you another," she reassures him, as if something so magical, so quickly and dearly loved, could be replaced without a second glance. "Don't cry!" she admonishes again a few years later when his puppy is hit by a car, and a few years after that when his first love gives back the friendship ring he spent his lawn-mowing money to buy and starts going out with his best friend. After that he never lets his mother see him cry again, which isn't hard since he doesn't do much of it anymore. Why don't we say to our children, "Cry! Cry! Cry!" since their lives are filled with losses and the capacity for mourning these marks them as human?

Having been effectively if not intentionally forbidden the expression of grief, we are bound to flounder emotionally in the face of tragedy as bitter as the loss of somebody's child. As a consequence, mourners sometimes experience very real, though generally inadvertent, cruelty. "I just wouldn't know what to say," people excuse themselves, scribbling a signature on a store-bought card, perhaps ordering an arrangement of lilies or roses to be delivered, and "after all, it's the thought that counts." But mourners may feel abandoned when friends avoid personal contact altogether or chatter brightly about anything but the dead child. Even words intended to be consolatory, often blurted out in embarrassment, can sting: "Miscarriages happen all the time, and anyway you can try again," as though this lost baby had no specific value. "At least she was too little to suffer very much," as though the younger the child, the less fully human. "Be thankful you have other children," as though any one of them could take the place of any other. "God must have wanted another little angel." Oh, yuck! Who came up with the idea that words of sympathy ought to instruct or inspire, as though one were addressing not a suffering soul but a football rally or a revival?

As a society, we have no legitimate form for directly expressing and sharing grief. Once again my thoughts are drawn back to Zaire, this time not to my own experience but to Anne's. Biko, the son of one of the farmers in Anne's village, a promising young man in his twenties who had sickle-cell anemia, went into a crisis. A truck was located and he was driven in it to the little hospital in Gombe-Matadi, about forty kilometers away, to be treated by the Belgian doctor there. Because Anne's was the only compatible blood type, a pint of her blood was quickly drawn and transfused into Biko. Although he had responded to this treatment before, this time his illness had advanced too far. He lay on a bed in the large room that served as the men's ward; in the shadows beyond the light of a single kerosene lantern, invisible patients coughed and rustled. The little group huddled around him could do nothing now but listen to his moans until they ceased. Then Biko's body was loaded back into the truck and driven home. There the mamas assembled, Anne among them, chatting sociably. Every so often one would start to wail, rocking back and forth, and the others would join in. "And I rocked and cried right along with them!" Anne reported with a mixture of amusement and wonder at her uncharacteristic display of emotion. "It just felt right."

For people like Anne and me, this noisy outcry would not customarily feel right at all. Cultural context determines propriety, and we come from a puritanical heritage that values emotional restraint above almost every other virtue. We never, ever howl, not even in the privacy of childbirth, certainly not in a public setting like a funeral. On the whole, I would say, funeral directors have adopted our tradition. Their very title and function suggest that matters can't be left in the hands of potentially unruly mourners but need to be placed under control. We don't keep our dead at home (where they probably didn't die anyway) but pack them off to mortuaries for embalming and viewing or, in about a quarter of the cases, cremation. We visit the bereaved not in their living rooms but at designated hours in funeral parlors, where the decor tends toward pale, neutral tones, the light is diffuse and rosy, and muted music, generally devotional, plays in the background. With a press of the hand or, if the acquaintance is more intimate, a kiss of the cheek, we murmur brief consolatory phrases, stand around awkwardly, speak to the other mourners in a hush if at all, and slip out as soon as decency permits. Those of us who are Catholic may pray the rosary together, relieving ourselves of the need to converse. Sometimes the funeral or memorial service is held right here, or later in a church, where reserve also reigns: eyes downcast, any sobs muffled.

I don't mean to condemn these customs, which are usually carried out with goodwill, but simply to point out that they serve to damp down and distance feeling in a way that contributes to social comfort but does not necessarily address or alleviate grief. In fact, grief in our society tends to be perceived as antisocial, disruptive of and even dangerous to the pursuit of pleasure and plenty that defines "happiness" for the modern sensibility, and therefore to be put behind quickly in order to get on with life — as though it stood somehow *outside of* life. One of my students, Louise, once told me that a year earlier she had lost her sixteen-year-old daughter to toxic shock syndrome and, she confided apologetically, she was still grieving, though everyone told her she'd mourned long enough. "But, Louise," I said, "it's been only a year, and to some extent you'll grieve such a terrible loss forever." Thinking of my own daughter, then about the same age, I knew that eternity itself could not be long enough.

Louise's friends were not being deliberately cruel. Contemporary attitudes about mental hygiene really do suggest that mourning is a diseased state to be gotten over rather than a ceaseless process of coming to terms with loss. The proliferation of "grief and loss" counselors reinforces this notion of pathology and enables laypeople to distance themselves further from bereavement. Appalled and uncertain in the face of raw pain, they turn it — as they do their automobiles, their backed-up toilets, their taxes, their own bodies — over to specialists. I have no complaint with specialists, bereavement counselors among them, but only with the way in which reliance on them may encourage a sense of personal helplessness. One may indeed be so confounded by the Internal Revenue Code as to require expert assistance; but in matters of the heart, one is required to do the work oneself.

God knows one may make a proper botch of it, however earnest and honorable one's intentions. When more than fifty years ago my mother-in-law was delivered of a full-term stillborn boy, the doctor, a childhood chum of her husband, had him taken away—I don't know where—while she was still sedated. After months of cherishing him with the peculiar inward-dreaming intensity only pregnancy induces, she was never allowed to see him. She never held him. She never said goodbye. No one ever mentioned him to her. In a measure bordering on sadism, she was sent to the maternity ward for the rather lengthy convalescence called for in those days, and everyone carefully looked away from her empty arms. The thinking seemed to be that if no one mentioned her loss, she'd recover from it more quickly. No one offered bereavement counseling. To do so would have required acknowledging the bereavement everyone was so busy pretending hadn't taken place. When I joined the family about fifteen years later, I also joined the collusion of silence, believing with the others that any reference to the baby would only upset her. Only in her seventies did she begin to talk to us about the experience, shoving aside the weight of silence we had all heaped upon her all those years. At long last, I've begun to understand that my husband was not, in fact, an only child. He had a little brother, whom his mother has cherished and mourned since 1946. She is entitled to have her maternity fully represented.

Nowadays, thanks to the insistence of the women's movement that women need not have the life protected out of them, the family's experience might have been less emotionally suffocating. When the daughter of a friend was born at only five months' gestation, she lived just long enough for her parents to hold her and name her. Her body was placed in a tiny hand-fashioned coffin, which was buried solemnly, and she took her place in the family, a beloved absence between siblings Jared and Alice, who could, if they wished, refer to their sister instead of having to pretend, like George, that they were all there was.

The complicated responses of children to a sibling's death are often misconceived and therefore mishandled by grieving adults. George, at five, knew there was going to be a baby. Then there was a flurry of crying, and no baby materialized. No one explained to him what had happened. He was excluded from their sadness. I suppose they told themselves that he was too young to understand, that if they said nothing he'd soon forget all about a baby. But of course he couldn't exactly forget, any more than he could quite remember. His parents repeatedly voiced their regret at having an only child. Being that child, he could only experience himself as at once desperately loved and undesirable, inadequate, not at all what they had in mind. Had he been permitted a little brother, of whom he too had been deprived, their disappointment could have been laid at the door of death and not across his shoulders.

Basically, it doesn't matter how old the child is when the death occurs, whether he or she ever knows or can remember the dead sibling, how much he or she initially understands about the event. No matter how hard the parents may try to repress their sorrow and concentrate on the child(ren) left, traces of the loss remain in their psyches; even the child born after, who missed the calamity altogether, must cope with these. In short, a dead sibling does not vanish like smoke but takes a place, insubstantial but perfectly real, in the family constellation, whether acknowledged or not. The ones permitted to do so openly and naturally often grace their families with exceptional tenderness and warmth.

But oh, these words, even though squeezed out like bitter drops against the full resistance of my soul, still make the process sound less anguished than it must be. I am blessed: I do not know. I still have my children.* I have my grandchildren, whom I visited in the course of writing this essay. As Anne was preparing them for our arrival, Colin reminded her, "Granna uses a wheelchair."

"That's right, Granna uses a wheelchair because she can't walk."

"But she can still read to me," he replied, "because she's people." What a benison, to be taken as I am and used for what I can offer!

Because I can't do much else, I spent a good deal of time just watching and listening to the boys. With my eidetic memory, I can now replay vignettes in my head like videotape.

---

*At the time I wrote this essay my foster son Ron had not yet been murdered. I have elected not to revise this portion of the essay because it points to the ironic tension between writing and living. How naïve — even a little smug — these words sound in the light of the loss to come.

Tow-headed Colin, characteristically pensive, munches six of the Toy Story cookies I've bought him, one for each character, content, not asking for more. Trevor, honey-haired and round, wearing his perpetual beatific smile, dribbles a miniature soccer ball past my chair. Colin replies, when I ask if I may see the tower he's erected in his bedroom, "Of course you may," and he removes toys from my path as I roll down the hallway behind him. Trevor staggers across the backyard, his smile obscured by the giant pink beach ball in his arms. Worn out by a visit to a historical farm, Colin—whose twos are proving quite terrible—whines interminably on the way home, and I attend to the cacophony with the same irked appreciation I might accord a John Cage composition. Trevor —whose twos, whatever their nature, lie a year away—sleeps through the performance.

How fragile my grandmotherly bliss might be I know only too well. Friends lost one of their grandsons, Shane, born exactly a week before Colin, in a freak electrical accident before his first birthday, and they generously shared their grief with us, not an easy gesture in a society that considers reference to any death, but especially that of a child, a ghoulish solecism. This essay is, in a sense, Shane's legacy to a woman he never met. Thoughts of his death sadden but do not frighten me. Rather, they sharpen my awareness of Colin and Trevor—as of their parents, myself, our friends and relations, the strangers who drift in and out of lives—in the world, as they are, now. Whether they will go on living, and if so what will become of them, I cannot possibly foresee. Current auguries reveal one mean little shortstop (for the Red Sox, I hope) and the driver of an eighteen-wheeler, but these are likely to change. Through their deaths or—blessedly more likely—my own, I will have to relinquish them one day. Worrying about that now would only distract me from the task at hand: to rejoice in them, as in us all, one breath after another.

# The Death of the Other

ON a weekday evening last winter our daughter, Anne, and son-in-law, Eric, telephoned us from Denver. Since we talk to them every Sunday, a midweek call signals something out of the ordinary requiring consultation or commentary, like the time their son Colin, at about a year, slid off the bed and knocked out a front tooth. We had to spend some time reminiscing about The Various Misadventures of Anne and Matthew, many of them involving copious quantities of blood, in order to persuade Anne that she wasn't a terrible mother (or at least not the only terrible mother), and we then rejoiced that Colin was otherwise fine and at least he would grow another tooth in its place, unlike his maternal grandparents, who have had to be patched up with porcelain. These occasions serve to remind me that even though George and I are now biologically beside the point, we retain a certain oracular function.

"Raisa has leukemia," they told us. This medium-sized black dog of indeterminate lineage, adopted from the Humane Society when she was eight weeks old, had lived with them since the year before they were married. Because they traveled, sometimes for quite lengthy periods, she also spent quite a bit of time with us before they moved, and we too grew fond of her. Unusually intelligent and athletic, she had lately seemed lethargic. The veterinary oncologist they consulted after diagnosis had offered them chemotherapy, an initial

treatment at $250 followed by two capsules, which cost $1
apiece, every day; they might in this way keep her alive for a
year or so. Living on a medical resident's salary, with two little boys to feed and clothe, they weren't sure this was a wise
use of funds.

We concurred. Not long before, a colleague of George's
had spent a thousand dollars on chemotherapy for her cat,
who had died anyway but not before suffering a great deal.
Although the side effects of chemotherapy can be wretched
enough for human beings, at least they can understand the
reason for their misery and choose whether or not to endure
it. An animal must experience only incomprehensible tor-
ment. If the outcome promises to be a cure—a broken leg
mended, say, or a wound healed—then the bewilderment and
pain might seem justified. Raisa, now nine, appeared to have
little chance of complete recovery. All their money could buy
was perhaps a little more time. Mightn't it be more wisely
spent, I asked, if invested for the boys' education?

In the end, they opted for giving Raisa the best life they
could and then, when she appeared to be suffering, having her
euthanized. With a small dose of prednisone every day but no
other treatment, she perked up for several months before
suddenly falling gravely ill. Another consultation: Were they
acting precipitously, should they give her more time to rally?
"I have never regretted putting an animal down," George assured them, "but I have often regretted not doing it soon
enough."

"What shall we tell Colin?" Anne asked. "Trevor's too little to pay much attention to her, but Colin loves her."

"Tell him the exact truth," I said, drawing on childhood

experience. "Don't tell him she got sick or he'll panic every time he sneezes, and don't tell him she was put to sleep or he'll never close his eyes again! Tell him she got cancer and died."

The next day Anne took Raisa to the vet and cradled her while the vet slipped a needle into a vein. "She was gone so quickly!" Anne reported. "She almost seemed relieved." She was cremated and her ashes put in a small box of brushed steel. Several months later, the family scattered them in the mountains where she loved to hike.

This little drama, their first of its kind as a family but surely not their last, has been enacted over and over in my life for almost as long as I can remember. My first dog, when I was three and living on Truk, was a little mongrel pup called, for some reason lost with the deaths of my parents, Petey-Puss-the-Platypus. She "went mad," whatever that meant, and had to be hunted down by men with guns, my father among them, and shot. Soon we moved to Guam, where our neighbors, upon their return to the States, left with us a giant black Lab named Rochester, who tolerated us all but adored my father. When we too had to leave the dog behind after Daddy died, the people who took him reported that, no longer willing to eat, Rochester didn't live long. Thus my earliest memories hold a tangle of losses both human and animal, two of them abrupt and quite violent, which, in imparting a sense of death's inevitability, created in me a resignation that has expressed itself, in its most unwholesome form, as depression but also, in my later and better days, as repose.

We continued to keep pets as I grew up: at first a canary named Orange Pekoe, who was joined (and perhaps done in) by a striped tabby, Honeybun, and later Pegeen the Irish setter and, over time, several other cats. I also knew the pets of my aunts and uncles, just as I knew my cousins, and occasionally we visited a great-uncle who eked out a hardscrabble living on a farm in Maine, where he raised chickens, a couple of pigs, and even for a while a black Angus bull, all of them named for members of the family. Nancy was a sow. The town we lived in was sufficiently rural that the wealthiest citizens kept horses, especially hunters and polo ponies, and the poorest, chickens and perhaps the odd sheep or cow. The people across the road from us had, along with their dogs and horses, a pair of Australian fainting goats that really did, if sufficiently startled, keel right over. There was even a sort of town mascot, a basset hound named Fred who, straying from his grounds, would wander about until he encountered the local taxi, which had standing orders to carry him home.

George had also grown up with pets—a beagle named Skipper who, after chewing the leg of his father's easy chair, was sent to that final solution for so many, a "good home in the country," and Inky the stump-tailed black cat, veteran of an encounter with a heedlessly reversed auto. Not surprisingly, then, we acquired our first pet, a handsome blue cat called The Mino, soon after we were married. He vanished— cat-napped, I'm certain—before very long, but he was followed by many others of varying and often overlapping tenure. There were Ho Tei and Anna, a pair of seal-point Siamese, and later Balthasar, also seal-point, and lynx-point Gwydion the mighty hunter, who once brought me a peeled hard-boiled egg from some neighbor's picnic; the black-and-whites, Kitten Little, who left us for fatter pickings a block away, and the Princess Saralinda; calico Mimi and the spotted tabbies, rotund Burton Rustle and then Lionel Tigress, the only one so thoroughly and noisily mad that we finally took her back to the Humane Society; half-feral Winchester, a gigantic white longhair who lived past venerability into senescence; and the best beloved blacks, Katie and Freya and Bête Noire and Eclipse and Vanessa Bell and, most recently, Osiris and Osiris Too.

We'd have been satisfied with cats, but the children wanted dogs, too. We started with a beagle named Daffodil, a howler and nipper who soon had to be found a good home in the country, where I would cheerfully consign all her breed. After a couple of mongrel puppies escaped and were hit by cars, I decreed that we would have no more; but one night eight-year-old Anne crawled into my lap sobbing, "I n-n-need a d-d-dog," and soon Amaroq, a Lab–sheepdog cross, had moved in. There were also, rather briefly, Amelia Earhart and later Pinto. Now, though the children are long gone, we live with a corgi-cross called Lucky Pup and that *ne plus ultra* of dogdom, a black Labrador retriever, Bentley Barker. Over the years, our hospitality extended to rabbits, guinea pigs, rats and mice, snakes, a tankful of tropical fish, and even a tarantula, each one with a name and a distinct disposition.

The fact that I can produce this catalog, spanning more than fifty years, reflects just how integrally these beasts have been enfolded into my life. In this I replicate a reality far older than human history, for dogs appear to have been domesticated since Paleolithic times, initially, a common hypothesis holds, in a mutually beneficial working relationship: because of their superior speed and olfactory sense, dogs were used to track prey and guard encampments; in return, they received food and warmth. Cats, I'm amused to discover, weren't tamed until many millennia later (if, those of us who live with them might add, at all), and by their very existence they give the lie to any notion of reciprocal usefulness. Unless you've developed a yen for fresh mole, a cat's hunting prowess will serve you poorly; and far from warding off real and present danger, he will likely freeze and stare only at things you can neither see nor conjure and, judging from his appalled gaze, wouldn't want to if you could. In the underwater passageway at the Arizona–Sonora Desert Museum, nose to nose with a frolicking otter, essayist Lewis Thomas identified the true reason we seek out the company of animals: "We hanker after friends."

Just when I reach this point in the essay, George comes into the studio. "I've had a disaster," he says behind me, "and I think I'll have to go to the emergency room for some stitches." I pivot to find him dripping blood from his lip and chin. On their afternoon walk Bentley spied a cat, wound the leash around George's ankles, and took off, pitching him chin-first into the gravel.

"Well, at least you won't need a tetanus shot," I point out on our way to the hospital. Last winter when we brought Osiris Too home from the Humane Society, Bentley immediately chased him into the backyard, George in hot pursuit, and in the ensuing melee the cat bit George's middle finger, which swelled and reddened alarmingly, an infection that required him to spend a night in the hospital receiving antibiotics intravenously. A tetanus shot at that time has brought him right up to date.

Otherwise, the news was not great. He required six sutures in his chin and one inside his lower lip. Because a mandibular fracture required his jaw to be wired tightly shut, for the next weeks he spoke through clenched teeth and took liquid nourishment, squirted from a syringe through a flexible red tube inserted into a small gap at the back of his mouth. Bentley, of course, was delighted to have George get right down to his level in the alley, delighted to lick the blood and sweat dripping from him, perhaps hopeful that more such offerings will be showered on him in future. Delight characterizes Bentley's true nature. With friends like Bentley, life certainly never loses its luster.

"I'm still crazy about him," George said later, and of course he is. So am I, even though my initial intention of training him as an assistance dog has been thwarted, at least to date, because he does not condescend to perform any act that might be perceived as servile. But for George and me, as for most of us nowadays, the chief reason for inviting animals into our lives has little enough to do with hunting and herding and guarding, little enough to do even with warming our feet on winter evenings, and just about everything to do with receiving and absorbing the inarticulable affection for the mysterious other which overflows our hearts. No longer do we invest creatures—the cat, the jackal, the serpent, the calf— with godhood; but our unconscious, knowing that we once did, continues to be drawn to them. I have been fascinated by every beast in our household and fond of most of them. Some I have loved helplessly, passionately. From them I have learned to live without hope of requital since, whether or not animals have emotional lives (and I feel certain that they do), they certainly cannot be expected to respond to my passion in kind. After all, we're lucky enough to get such responses from our fellow human beings. Let's keep our expectations reasonable.

The failure to distinguish our own wishes, needs, and feelings from those of animals helps explain some of our society's silliest excesses. Take a trip to your nearest PETsMART if you want a dazzling illustration of these: several thousand square feet packed with goods and goodies for dogs, cats, birds, fish, rodents. *Rodents!* People who hire technicians to rid their houses of mice and squirrels then buy elaborate Habitrails to entertain their hamsters. Because dogs and cats are by far the most popular pets, the bulk of the merchandise is designed to house, entertain, clothe, and nourish them. Either inside or outside your own dwelling, they may occupy crates, igloos, baskets, or padded perches. Hundreds of balls, Frisbees, ropes, and bones encourage the canine preference for interactive retrieval and romping; the variety of furry dead things reflects the cat's solitary and predatory nature (though a couple of my cats trained me to play fetch). Halters, collars, leashes, sweaters, ponchos, and boots provide restraint and environmental protection. For feeding, specialized diets proliferate: formulas for puppies and kittens; youths; breeding, active, and sedentary animals; senior canine and feline citizens; and the overweight. People starve to death in huge numbers throughout the world, and we spend money helping pets shed the excess pounds we've packed onto them in the first place.

When Anne lived in Zaire, I recall, she drew criticism from

her neighbors because, since the ribs of her dog, Celeste, didn't show, she was obviously feeding her rather than letting her scrounge through the village and forest as the other dogs did—a blatant waste of resources. Although Anne went on giving Celeste and her cats small meals, she grew more sensitive over time. One afternoon while her friend Djili was visiting, one of the cats brought in an *mpuku* and began to toy with it. This small rodent, though considered unclean if found in the house, may be eaten when caught out of doors, and Anne noticed Djili watching it with interest. She was probably wondering whether this *mundele* (white person) was going to feed this perfectly good meal to her cat. By then, however, Anne knew enough to ask, "Would you like to take the *mpuku* for your dinner?" The offer quickly accepted, Anne retrieved the *mpuku* unharmed and Djili took it home for her family. Upon her return to the States, Anne left her pets with the teenage boys who had worked for her. Since they were fond of Celeste, she thought the dog might survive, but she was pretty sure the cats would wind up in a pot with palm oil, garlic, onions, tomatoes, and hot red *pili pili* (peppers).

I am of, not above, my society. I go to PETsMART. Although, compared with a poodle in Manhattan, Bentley is a cheap date, I buy him lamb-and-rice kibble and squeaky toys and a woven collar and leash in colors that complement his glossy black coat. I have no plans for eating him. But neither do I live in a part of the world where protein is so scarce that a good-sized fruit bat is considered a delicacy. ("What did it taste like," people ask when I say I've eaten *ngembo*, "chicken?" "No," I have to say, "bat.") Thanks to Anne, I understand that keeping a dog well fed, well groomed, and healthy is a mark of privilege. I spend several hundred dollars on Bentley every year, more than enough to have supported Ma Charlotte and Tata Vita and their burgeoning brood in Zaire at the time I met them. Looking at Bentley this way, I have to wonder whether I am entitled ethically to the luxury of his friendship. If I elect to keep it, I do so at the expense of whatever starving people might have been fed had I spent the money otherwise.

We do animals no service by imagining them to be people like us dressed up in furry, feathery, or scaly costumes and expecting them to relate to us accordingly. This kind of projection can even lead to unintentional abuses. For example, because my mother-in-law's idea of a treat is a sweet, as she ate a cookie she always broke off bits and slipped them to her dog under the table. In this way, she trained Vicky to hang around while people were eating and beg for handouts, a behavior unlikely to endear her to a good many diners. To further diminish Vicky's charms, the sugar caused her teeth to decay and eventually fall out and her breath to reek. Although we haven't had much trouble training our dogs to go to their beds while we eat, it took *years* to break Mum of slipping them goodies when we weren't looking, and I suspect she still thinks we don't love our animals as much as she loved hers because we don't share our own food with them.

Some people "love" creatures not just into bad manners and bad breath but into downright danger. They may adopt more pets than they can take care of adequately. They may capture wildlife without knowing how to meet its needs; or they may "free" pets to roam at will, risking accidents and disease, and to express their sexual selves by reproducing indiscriminately. Several years ago members of the Animal Liberation Front released several hundred experimental animals from laboratories at the University of Arizona without apparent regard for the diets they may have required or the diseases they may have been carrying. (They also burned down a house across the street from mine, where laboratory records were being stored, thereby jeopardizing the animals living with me.) Although some animal rights activists argue that animals should not even be kept as pets, the fact is that if they are fed appropriately and exercised regularly, most animals lead safer and healthier lives with us than without us. That's why they domesticated us in the first place, so as to have a reliable source of kibble and fresh water and a place to get in out of the rain.

The firebugs of the Animal Liberation Front were protesting the use of animals in scientific experiments, an issue about which I feel some ambivalence. I am well aware that animals are often exploited in order to indulge human caprice. No one *needs* fur coats made from bludgeoned baby harp seals, cosmetics tested in the eyes of rabbits, pure-white veal (or any meat at all), a day out at the dog track or the bull fights. I can't imagine anyone but a sybarite or a sadist arguing in favor of such goods and practices. Even allowing for the hyperbole to which activists are prone, some laboratory experiments, as well as the conditions under which they are conducted, may be too atrocious to condone. More troublingly, the results of such experiments may not even reveal precisely what researchers want to know: how a given procedure or drug will affect the human body.

Mice, the most common research animals, do not contract

multiple sclerosis, but a demyelinating syndrome which causes similar symptoms can be induced. Experimental allergic encephalomyelitis, or EAE, provides a model of MS which researchers have used extensively for exploring the progress of and potential treatments for the disease. Neurological dysfunction causes symptoms disagreeable enough that I wouldn't lightly wish them on *Drosophila melanogaster* (whose rights I have never heard defended), let alone a mouse. Nevertheless, if the use of mice can speed discoveries that might lead to better management of MS—even, perhaps, a cure—I'm all for enlisting their aid, as long as the EAE model is demonstrably preferable to some other technique and the animals are well cared for, thereby privileging my own well-being over that of another species. As with my keeping Bentley, I may do as I will but I must remain conscious that I am accepting an ethically questionable practice.

Although privileging myself over little white whiskered rodents may mark me as "speciesist," I don't think the same is true when we simply draw distinctions between ourselves and our fellow creatures. On the contrary, by attributing human needs, motivations, and responses to other animals, we fail to acknowledge and respect their individual and mysterious creatureliness. We pretend to know the world they live in, as though they lived in a single world that conforms in every way to ours instead of a multiplicity of alien territories inaccessible to our senses. I would not presume to comprehend the topographical complexities mapped by Bentley's nose on one of our afternoon walks, any more than I expect him to know why I peck at this keyboard while he drowses beside me. We are entitled to our own lives.

* * *

And to our deaths as well, each kind mourning the other in its own way. Whether or not animals possess consciousness or experience emotion, a signal difference separates Bentley qua beast from me even though we both possess animal nature. I know what Bentley cannot: that no matter how I coddle him, he will grow old and feeble and die, probably at about age twelve; that either before or after him, I will do the same. Perhaps if he could reflect upon his own end, he would cease to be a dog and become a person. Perhaps knowledge of death is what makes a being human.

They say that pets and their owners look alike. I have my doubts about this adage. A friend with alopecia who used to keep Afghan hounds may have admired their long, silken tresses but certainly could never hope to grow any of his own. And Bentley is far handsomer than either George or me. Nevertheless, I do think that the pets we choose (or permit to choose us) and the way we relate to them often reflect truths about our inner lives that would be hard to get at by other means. Certainly, we can learn much about our attitudes toward suffering and death from the way we respond to their dying.

Over the years, I have grieved the disappearance of many a small creature, kept a death watch over many more, converted pillow slips into winding sheets, officiated at many a graveside farewell. Of all the losses, the death of the little black cat Vanessa Bell a couple of years ago was perhaps the most moving for George and me. Not that we were surprised by it, since hyperthyroidism had been burning away her flesh for many months, until at the end she was a mere bundle of bones clothed in tatters of fur. Nevertheless, her departure gouged a hole in our hearts bigger than the one George dug for her body. Toward the end we took to feeding her salmon in aspic and permitting her to snitch tidbits from our plates, two foolish old people indulging their beloved beast in her last days. At seventeen she had lived with us for half our married lives, sleeping every night in the crook of my knee or on George's pillow. She was one of our Humane Society rescues, a skittish scrap of a thing, half-Siamese, whose voice grew bigger than she ever did.

As she aged, she grew more sociable, and when the Community of Christ of the Desert met in our home for worship, she would often join us, circling the room to be petted and yowling along with our hymns. If there were ailurophobes among us, they were too polite to say so. I've been wary of allowing our pets in the house during the liturgy ever since, when someone dropped a bit of the Host, Lucky Pup snapped it up, becoming perhaps the only corgi ever to have made his first communion. Reluctant to offend our more traditional members, we have banished the dogs. But except for the singing, Vanessa Bell seemed inclined less to participate in our celebration than to grace it with her presence.

In Christianity, the beasts have no souls, which are reserved for the beings created in God's own image (the very ones, perhaps not coincidentally, who scripted this story of their creation). By virtue of believing themselves to have what other creatures have not, human beings claim "dominion over the fish of the sea, and over the birds of the air, and over the cattle, and over all the wild animals of the earth, and over every creeping thing that creeps upon the earth."

Adopting this superior stance reflects, ironically, one of our least human qualities, as anyone who has lived with a couple of dogs can attest: their interactions involve almost exclusively who gets to be on top of whom.

That Vanessa Bell should have lacked a soul troubles me very little, since I don't believe in the "soul" as it is conventionally understood, a perdurable entity that will one day depart the body and travel either "up" or "down" depending on the quality of that body's brief being. This strikes me as the sort of magical tale children concoct to talk themselves out of inexpressible terrors. What prospect can appall, at any age, more than annihilation? No wonder we cling to the certainty that although the body demonstrably dies and decays, some separable element endures. Nothing is "wrong" about this belief. On the contrary, I have seen it provide immeasurable comfort. I simply don't share it.

Yet the little heap of bones clad in its black rags was unquestionably not the Vanessa Bell to whom, not long before, I bade goodbye and Godspeed. Something indeed seemed to have "gone out" of her, something precious that made her herself and not a piece of quartz or a featherbush or even one of those dozen or so other cats who have owned us over the years, though the same elements compose them all. Call it vital force. Call it breath. Call it spirit. Call it, perhaps most aptly, anima, that which made her, as it makes us, animal.

For the most part, Vanessa Bell was nothing like me. But "nothing like" does not suggest "inferior to." Hers was a feline spirit, mine a human one, but the Spirit subsumes us both. I'm sure God doesn't sit above, as human beings like to do, preferring one element of creation over another. God *is* creation through and through: the All of It, present always and everywhere, immersed in the process of ever coming into being. Unlike some of my New England forebears, I am no transcendentalist; call me, rather, an immanentist. I bear God into the world, as did Vanessa, as do the Santa Catalina Mountains to my north and the Crab Nebula far beyond my view. We constitute the glory of God; and if human beings too often do so badly, the more fools we.

Both blessed and cursed by intellect, as Vanessa was not, I have meandered some way from her little corpse, shrouded in a pillowcase, which rests under the privet outside my gate. In the eighteenth century, a mad poet named Christopher Smart wrote a jumbled, baffling, but frequently brilliant poem entitled "Jubilate Agno," one part of which celebrates his cat Geoffrey. "For I am possessed of a cat surpassing in beauty," this reads, "from whom I take occasion to bless Almighty God." After the years of generous nuzzles and purrs and finger-nibbles, of spilt pitchers and bird feathers behind the toilet, Vanessa—like her predecessors of every stripe and spot—made me this parting gift: an occasion for praise.

# Reflections on an Anniversary

HALLOWEEN is coming round again. Not that you'd know it in Tucson, where we have had the second hottest September on record—unless, like me, you'd lived here a very long time. "Oh, don't you miss the seasons?" people ask, as though I lived in the heart of an equatorial jungle rather than a northern temperate desert. Actually, as far as I'm concerned, every day of the year could be sunny and eighty-five degrees. I wouldn't get bored. I notice that those most solicitous of my seasonal deprivation are the ones who endure the most appalling extremes: humid, buggy summers, dark winters smothered in snow followed by spring's sucking mud. I do not miss most of it. Except for autumn: the flare of foliage in crystalline air dying, as light fails, into umber and gray. Except for Halloween.

The truth is that the seasons change in Tucson, too, although the signals are different and often subtler than at more northerly latitudes. We have summer rains (dubbed "monsoon" season), when moisture from the south, heated by the scorched desert floor, blooms in chrysanthemums of clouds trailing ribbons of lightning and rain. We have winter rains, pulsing across from the Pacific Coast every few days with a load of rain or, occasionally, snow. We even had a white Christmas once. Depending on how early and plenteously these rains fall, the desert may be carpeted with lupine and California poppies in the spring; but even in the worst years, at least some of the cactuses and succulents flare great showy blossoms in yellow, vermilion, purple, and white. And even though the thermometer is still climbing toward 100 degrees and we had a spectacular thunderstorm yesterday, I know that fall has replaced summer by a faint and tantalizing crispness to the morning air and the slant of the light as the sun swings south. No matter how persistent the heat, common wisdom has it, the cold (such as it is) will come by Halloween.

Thus Halloween marks for us, as it did for the Celts in whose propitiatory festival it may have roots, the end of summer. The belief of these ancient people that the souls of the dead returned to their homes on this night may have persisted after their conversion, so that All Hallows' Eve, the night before All Saints' Day in the Christian liturgical year, took on an association with "ghoulies and ghosties" that Pope Gregory IV, in declaring November 1 a churchwide solemnity in the ninth century, seems unlikely to have intended. Nor would he have anticipated the mingling, more than half a millennium later, of Aztec belief in the annual return of dead souls with the faith brought by Spanish missionaries to create El Día de Los Muertos celebrated in Mexico, and thus by many in our area just north of the border, at this time of year. Part of Christianity's genius for survival has always lain in its capacity to enfold (and often smother) whole belief systems and transform them to its own ends, thereby enriching its symbols and practices immeasurably.

Catholics are still instructed to observe All Saints' Day, as well as All Souls' Day on November 2, and to devote the whole month to reflections on mortality. In Mexican culture, entire families may still repair to the cemetery to clean the crypts and monuments of their dear departed and erect altars

decorated with marigolds and *ofrendas* of food, drink, cigarettes, and anything else they believe the dead may enjoy in
spirit (and they will later relish in truth). But for most people
in the United States, death and its "victims" get short shrift at
this as at other times of year. Indeed, Halloween, now thoroughly secularized and commercialized, has been turned over
to children (and to adults replaying the childhood game of
dress-up). The evil spirits against whom the Celts lit their
hilltop bonfires, now diminutive and round-cheeked, trudge
through well-lighted streets (where they are safe doing so) or
gather in more protected but noisier indoor spaces clutching
cheerful plastic jack-o'-lanterns full of sweets, and if our dead
are represented at all, they dress in cast-off sheets and giggle
when they shout "Boo!" Having relegated the festivities to
the realm of children, whom we naturally want to spare at
least half the experiences they must have in order to become
human, we can—socially speaking—avoid contemplating
our mortality even once a year.

All the same, as vegetation shrivels and days shorten, some
druidic dread may still stir in the human unconscious. Perhaps the coming chill and the autumnal dying of the light help
explain why, in a life tinted by depression's drab tones, I have
more than once found myself in acute trouble at this time of
year. Or perhaps I have tried to kill myself in the fall purely by
coincidence. Whichever way, I am mindful just now that this
Halloween, twenty years will have passed since my last suicide attempt. Not that I chose Halloween as my night to end it
all. It happened to fall on a Friday night that year. Otherwise,
I'd have a different anniversary. But in retrospect, I like the
choice.

In retrospect, I suppose that the event, if not the particular date, was inevitable. Although I had not had a major depressive episode since spending seven months in a mental hospital in the late 1960s, I had been coming undone for a long time, probably since quitting my medication when I got pregnant with my second child. Because the symptoms of agoraphobia that had once confined me had abated, though they would never entirely disappear, I didn't recognize that I was spiraling into another crisis. The signs can be so subtle — and sometimes so silly. I took to sitting on the edge of my bed, staring into my closet, unable to decide what to put on before dragging myself through another day. Yet I never actually went naked. My desks at home and at school developed middens of books, papers, and the other detritus of an academic life, making efficient work impossible. Yet I both taught and attended classes regularly, prepared lessons and graded papers, turned in my own assignments on time. My house grew ever more dirty and dilapidated, but no one got food poisoning and no one was standing underneath when the dining-room ceiling fell in. Who was to say that I wasn't just fine?

In the summer of 1980, my dissolution picked up speed. I returned from my first writers' conference dissatisfied with a life I had crammed too full of other duties to leave me time for writing yet incapable of envisioning any other kind of life. I resumed keeping a journal, a professional practice in most writers' lives but in mine, ironically, a danger signal. Most tellingly, I began an extramarital affair with yet another in a long string of men even more unavailable emotionally than I was in fact. By August I could no longer sleep through the night. Though never petite, by September I weighed ninety-five pounds and fit into size 5 clothes. Abruptly announcing to my baffled family that I needed my own space, I moved into a one-room apartment a few blocks away, returning to visit them on weekends. At this point, I still didn't recognize what was happening to me, although I agreed to take the antidepressant my neurologist prescribed.

I knew so little about depression in those days. Doctors withheld or distorted information. For instance, the Harvard-trained psychiatrist who treated me for five years at the time of my first breakdown told me that I had no reason to expect to have another, although in fact the odds markedly favored a recurrence; nor did he present depression as a potentially chronic condition requiring biochemical correction for the rest of my life. Maybe he was trying to reassure me, or maybe (and this was more his style) he didn't want to put any ideas into my silly little noodle. In any case, that bit of deceit led me to think myself immune to further problems, as though I'd recovered from the chicken pox, and so to scant symptoms for which I might otherwise have sought help. When I finally did so, my neurologist failed to warn me—perhaps did not even know—that as the antidepressant took effect, the risk of suicide would rise temporarily but sharply. I thought the mere gesture of swallowing the little yellow pills made me safe.

Until that Halloween when I deliberately swallowed a great many of them at once. And I mean "deliberately." I was no raving maniac throughout this period. Except for the night that my "lover" broke off relations with me, when I lay on my narrow bed and howled for hours, I remained lucid and in control. The howling, which continued inside without cease, never again broke through. My demeanor, though it must have been sad, was never frantic enough to arouse anyone's

concern. I never threatened suicide. Had Jack Kevorkian in-
terviewed me at that time, I think I could have convinced him
that I had simply reached a level of pain so intense that my life
was no longer worth living; but I sought no one's assistance.
Alone with my little black cat, without fear, without any feeling at all except the incessant shrieking anguish, I methodi-
cally downed many too many pills—the means women are
said to prefer. Had I been a man with a gun . . .

When I roused eighteen hours later and George, who had
tracked me down, hauled me into the emergency room, I told
the psychiatrist there that I was no longer depressed, and really I wasn't, not in the way I had been. My misery persisted,
and would persist for quite a long time, but death no longer
seemed the only possible measure in response to it. Instead, I
might—however grimly—endure. A friend once speculated
that I no longer needed to commit suicide because I had died
symbolically if not in fact. In a more medical than metaphori-
cal frame of mind, I have always theorized that by taking what
could have been a lethal dose but clearly in my case was not, I
booted myself straight out of despair, achieving a biochemical
balance sufficient to permit me to function over the long term
as a clinical depressive with suicidal tendencies without suc-
cumbing to death's blandishments.

However one explains my survival, I have had two decades
of the life I sought to discard, and on the whole I don't regret
a moment of them, even though the "quality" of that life—as
that phrase is now conventionally understood—has deteriorated steadily. Then, I was still a youngish and independent
woman. Diagnosed with multiple sclerosis eight years earlier,
I walked with a brace and cane and had recently acquired a

scooter for distances. Nevertheless, as a doctoral student I carried a full load of teaching and course work. My MS figured as a nuisance, slowing down and complicating but not preventing my routine. Over the years I have lost the ability to work, to drive, to walk, to put on or take off my clothes, to turn over in bed, even to pee. With each new indignity, I think I've come to the end of my endurance, and then I get through another day.

A couple of years ago, I met one of my husband's colleagues who also has MS. Complaining of the fatigue that is perhaps the peskiest symptom of this disease, he said he was so exhausted at the end of a teaching day that he fell into bed as soon as he got home and didn't drag himself out again until the next morning.

"Why don't you get a wheelchair, Jay," I asked, "so you'd have some energy left for important things?" Like your wife and children, I thought, who must be reaping small joy from your prone and suffering form.

"You'll see me dead first," he replied. I was startled and a little amused. This man had just looked straight at me and said, in so many words, that I'd be better off dead than tooling around campus in my little black power chair. Some days I might well agree with him, but this didn't happen to be one of them. I felt a frisson of fear for him.

"You sound awfully depressed," I said. "Have you tried any medication?"

"I can handle my life without relying on pills." This stiff-upper-lipness, characteristic of but hardly exclusive to men who have invested heavily in manly attitudes and activities, ill befits either cripples or depressives. Jay had always prized himself as an athlete, George had told me. Now, instead of forging a new identity to replace the one "spoiled" by MS (to use social theorist Erving Goffman's term), he seemed intent upon quitting the game altogether.

"Maybe so," I replied, "but without antidepressants I wouldn't be alive today." This statement always sounds overblown to me, even though it's true. I've lived these twenty years because I take mood-elevating drugs. These, despite the hopeful phraseology, don't make me "high." Indeed, I can't tell that I'm taking them at all. More dangerously, I can't tell that I'm *not* taking them. George has learned to pick up the earliest signals—a flattened tone, an indirect gaze—but these are so subtle, and I've grown so accomplished at masking them, that those who know me less well would likely have no chance to intervene.

For this reason, I have come to think of taking antidepressants not as a failure to handle my life but as a means of taking responsibility for it and for the well-being of those, like George, who sometimes seem to value it more dearly than I do. I have never made peace with the fact that I came perilously close to killing myself one Halloween when my children were too old for trick-or-treating and more than old enough to pick up the unspoken message that their mother was willing to die and leave them. If I require pills to keep me from sinking into the kind of pathological self-absorption that act reflects, hand me the bottle.

But can I be trusted with the bottle? It contains an antidepressant very like the one that nearly killed me; and although it has proved remarkably efficacious when taken at appropriate dosages, it isn't foolproof. More important, should I be trusted with it? If not, whose task is it to see that I take my medication as prescribed and don't squirrel it away "just in case"? Are my "guardians" at fault if I elude their vigilance and kill myself in spite of it? What ought they to do if I tell them my life has become unbearable, because of MS or some other physical deterioration, and I would like their assistance in ending it? Are they guilty of cruelty if they deny me surcease? Of complicity if they uncap the bottle my hands are too weak to grasp, shake out the pills, pour me a glass of water, hold it to my lips? Ought they to be punished? How, and by whom?

The very asking of these questions might be deemed heretical in some quarters, among them the Catholic church, whose faith I embraced more than twenty years ago. For centuries "self-murderers" have been denied burial in consecrated ground and consigned (though surely not by God) to eternal damnation. My qualms about suicide don't spring from fear for my immortal soul, however, since I am one of those commonly sneered at as "cafeteria" Catholics. (In view of the outrages committed in God's name throughout church history—burning women as witches, leading little children to certain death, condemning Jews as "Christ-killers," whipping oneself bloody—and of the glories of art, architecture, music, and literature produced in God's praise, I think one ought to pick and choose among the church's doctrines with considerable care.) I make no apology, then, for believing that God expects us, as what theologian Matthew Fox calls God's "co-creators," to sort through moral issues one by one, teasing out their full consequences and implications, rather than following, like docile children, a set of rules, obedience to which may sometimes, but not invariably, result in right action. As attested by incidents like the shootings of doctors who perform abortions, adherence to a moral absolute can lead just as easily to atrocity.

We would all like our moral lives to be far simpler than they are. This desire, like so many others, is a holdover from our earliest days, when we relied on parents to reward us consistently for "good" behavior and chastise us for "bad." The infant in us, though overlaid by later developmental stages, remains alive and squalling in our deepest recesses, impulsive, easily startled, uncertain how to behave in unfamiliar circumstances, frantic for structure in a world wholly beyond our control. Small wonder that we create God in the image of the large and mysterious beings whose dictates calm our chaos. But unless we are cognitively damaged, we grow beyond the fearful worship of parental omnipotence. Indeed, many of us loom large and mysterious in the psychic lives of new beings, whom we give what direction we can until they, too, achieve adulthood. We are none of us helped in this process by worshiping an Almighty Father who so regiments our spiritual lives that we can fly on automatic pilot straight through them to salvation.

I cannot say absolutely, then, that suicide is either right or wrong but only: "It depends." My abortive suicide twenty years ago now strikes me as wrong because, in addition to acting when I was mentally deranged, I planned and carried out my attempt in secret. Most suicides occur under this condition, not merely in order to prevent others from intervening, I think, but because when depression is deepest, one loses all sense of human attachment. Suicide is then an unwilled but utter failure of love, its consequences invariably cruel. My physical condition has deteriorated even as my mental illness has been ameliorated by talk therapy, an ever more sophisticated psychopharmacopeia, spiritual practice, and plain old advancing years; and I have come to consider suicide in a different light, not as a clandestine and desperate act but as a means of sparing myself and those I love from undue effort and expense in postponing my inevitable end.

Suicide in the abstract is thus both right and wrong; only in individual cases may the one quality prevail over the other. Specifically, like other major choices, suicide's risks and merits are difficult to weigh; and, because at an inchoate level human nature shies away from ambiguity, we endeavor to reduce such dilemmas to a simpler, more definite structure. To this end, we become legalistic, placing our trust in an external Word instead of our own powers of discernment. Recent controversies over whether to pass laws permitting physician-assisted suicide clearly illustrate this urge to specify publicly a single clear-cut rule that will relieve us of the anguish of thinking through, and then bearing full responsibility for, decisions about life's most fundamental issues (and death too is a *life* issue).

I'm not recommending that we abolish or flout laws. I'm awfully glad, for instance, that we've all agreed (well, almost all) to stop our vehicles at red lights rather than weigh the merits and consequences of our actions at every intersection. I object only when I perceive the law proliferating in areas that belong properly in the moral domain, thereby constricting and occasionally perverting our capacity for true justice. The Jesus of the Gospels illustrates the transition I have in mind from Mosaic law to individual conscience—replicated in the psychic dimension of each of us—in the narrative of the woman caught in adultery. "In the law Moses commanded us to stone such," the scribes and the Pharisees say to him, challenging him to say otherwise. Without disputation, Jesus replies, "Let the one among you who is without sin be the first to throw a stone at her." At issue is not the adultery itself, against which he cautions in several other Gospel passages, but the locus of responsibility. When the law-enforcers have to scrutinize their own souls, they slink away. Jesus refuses to condemn the woman without condoning her deed. Instead, he places the power of right action squarely with the wrongdoer: "Go, and do not sin again." Does she comply? Who knows. But in his parting injunction, Jesus has conferred upon her (a woman, no less!) moral adulthood, the capacity to choose, in future, to refrain from iniquity.

Is suicide—one's own or aid in another's—similarly sinful? After all, the Mosaic code forbids killing as plainly as it forbids adultery. But is all bringing-to-death "killing"? Apparently not, since many people, among them the most fervent "Christians," decry abortion as the killing of unborn children yet hail execution as a murderer's just deserts. Since both measures are lawful, obviously legality cannot determine their propriety. Once again, every deed must be scrutinized in its own context, and in some instances killing oneself to end unbearable suffering might be justified and helping another to this end might indeed constitute an act of mercy, even of love.

Many seem to think that assisted suicide is a recent development, but of course it has occurred throughout human history, and doubtless prehistory as well. What's novel about it, as about so many personal matters, is its eruption into the public sphere. In a society where the dimensions and distinguishing characteristics of the president's penis can be speculated upon not merely in the boudoir or at intimate dinner parties, where gossip has always abounded, but by self-appointed and/or self-serving pundits in the national media, so that the complexion of all the "press" has turned a sickly yellow, no issue is presumed to be handled more appropriately in private. As my writing demonstrates, I don't oppose public discussion of all kinds of subjects if revelation promotes the general welfare (though I would just as soon shroud the body parts). But public decision-making is quite different from discussion. If at some point I choose to end my life, I want to do so in consultation with my family, my doctors, and my spiritual advisers, but I want lawyers and newsmongers kept strictly outside the loop.

The possibility of choosing to end my life implies the equal and opposite possibility of choosing not to do so, and I am exquisitely aware that there are those who might find such a choice puzzling at the least, even downright improper. As a person with a disability, I am assumed by many to lead a life without worth, and plenty of them would be glad to help me end my misery. Medical personnel, trained to heal bodily ills, are especially apt to view people like me, who have chronic, often incurable conditions, as "hopeless." Some neurologists, for instance, refuse to take patients with MS, or voice their distaste for such patients, as though the neurological syndrome were equivalent to the person. People with disabilities report being required to sign do-not-resuscitate forms in order to receive treatment in hospital.

Because many of us can't hold jobs, and those who can are too rarely offered them, in a culture that commonly confounds social value with economic productivity our lives are often considered worthless. More chillingly, they are characterized as drains on resources, both public and private, which could better be spent on more deserving projects than the upkeep of our wretched bodies. One of Jack Kevorkian's clients, I've heard, was told repeatedly by her husband that she was a vampire sucking his blood. In most cases such verbal assault would be deemed a type of domestic abuse. In hers it led to justification for her suicide.

Dr. Kevorkian's name comes up in my deliberations because his actions have rendered rational discourse about assisted suicide all but impossible. To begin with, he is a pathologist by training and inclination, a man who appears to have been fascinated from an early age by death. Though without credentials in psychotherapy, pastoral care, or even medicine (having lost his license years ago), he claims to "counsel" those who put themselves into his hands. The longest he has known one of these is a couple of months; in one case, he provided his service in less than twenty-four hours. He does not consult physicians, counselors, or spiritual advisers (on behalf of either his clients or himself). His messianic zeal for his self-appointed task (and perhaps for the attendant publicity) has earned him the moniker "Dr. Death."

Of the hundred and thirty people whose deaths Kevorkian

claims to have taken part in, the majority have been women, many with multiple sclerosis. Hardly surprising, then, that I find his work particularly alarming! Even more unsettling, some have had no clear diagnosis at all. In his determination, however, the quality of these sufferers' lives has become "nil" and he is merely terminating their misery. That this might have been terminated by other means—mood-elevating drugs and painkillers, financial aid, adequate assistance with personal care, meaningful day-to-day activities, a supportive community, even in some cases a pet—isn't likely to occur to a pathologist, who by definition devotes himself to the study of disease, not to its melioration. Indeed, some of Kevorkian's remarks reveal a sense of himself as a social hygienist, purging humanity of waste matter.

A great many people with disabilities like their lives a lot. So far, I happen to be one of them. We tend to repudiate the medical model of disability, which views us as sick and in need of a cure, and the mechanical model, in which we are broken and require repair. We see disability rather as a social construction, in which the assumptions and insensitivities of the majority assign limits, not merely differences, to bodies and minds that work in "deviant" ways. Some would go so far as to say that society at large is responsible for dis-abling us, that with plenty of ramps, Braille, interpreters, and other modifications, we would live just as easily in the world as anyone else.

In my experience a certain amount of suffering attends disability regardless of how well it is accommodated. Even though I have been spared the physical agony that attends some conditions, I am plagued by a host of niggling discomforts. Emotionally, even when not depressed, I feel inexpressibly sad. I long to the point of pain to scoop up my little grandsons, cuddle them, rock them, play pat-a-cake and peekaboo, trot them on my knee to Boston, to Lynn, just as my Granna did with me. No anodyne can ease my grief that my arms and legs have grown too weak for romping. I yearn to perform all kinds of tasks no longer possible for me, even — some people might find this really sick — ironing. I'm fed up with my wheelchair, my swollen feet, my suprapubic catheter, the injection of interferon I take every other night, and with all the extra work these items create for my caregivers. I just want to be able to scratch my own mosquito bites. Some of my limitations stem from nothing except my MS, and I must come to terms with them or . . . die.

Perhaps because I have embraced a faith with crucifixion at its heart, I do not consider suffering an aberration or an outrage to be eliminated at any cost, even the cost of my life. It strikes me as an element intrinsic to the human condition. I don't like it. I'm not asked to like it. I must simply endure in order to learn from it. Those who leap forward to offer me aid in ending it, though they may do so out of the greatest compassion, seek to deny me the fullness of experience I believe I am meant to have.

I'm not a masochist. I do not wish to end my days in teeth-gnashing excruciation. I have no reason to expect to do so, however. Because of my intimate association with cancer patients, many of whom I have accompanied through their dying, I know that with responsible pain management and responsive companionship, we tend to leave life with rather more dignity than we entered it. Part of the public hue and cry over assisted suicide springs from sheer ignorance about death, resulting in such terror that we seek to bring it on prematurely and under our own control so as not to risk either pain or helplessness. Because we ship the dying off to "healthcare facilities" instead of keeping them among us, most of us never learn to view death as one of life's major events, to be planned for and seen through with a different spirit but no less care than a wedding, a birth. We need to spend time with the dying in order to gain the wisdom to go through the same process ourselves—as every one of us will do—with grace.

"To comfort the dying" is one of the seven corporal works of mercy, but no particular manner of death is specified or excluded. As for those who are ready and determined to die on their own terms, then, let them have their will. "Take her home," the psychiatrist told George in the emergency room twenty years ago. "I think she'll be all right. But if she wants to kill herself, she will no matter what. They always do." Too often in doing so, however, they both endure and inflict egregious distress that candid discussion and medical support could ease if not eliminate.

Whenever I argue that legislation is an inappropriate tool for resolving our quandaries about suicide, invariably someone bursts out, "Oh, but we have to have a law to prevent people from killing indiscriminately." Maybe your acquaintance extends to villains and thugs, doctors who slip lethal chemicals into veins and then harvest organs to sell on the black market, scions who smother bedridden parents in order to hasten their inheritance, but mine doesn't. Such acts are possible but rare. They seem dreadfully common because the media seize and worry them with the relish of rat terriers, so that a single incident may bombard us for weeks, even months. Because human intelligence depends on our capacity to generalize, even when we lack adequate evidence, and since our odds for survival may improve when we expect the worst, we tend to assume that others must be committing similar atrocities without getting caught. A case constitutes "only the tip of the iceberg," we say, and so we ban the behavior it illustrates on the grounds "better safe than sorry" (generalization often leading to platitudes).

Far from being bloodthirsty fiends, most people who enter medicine seek to cheat death, not to court it. If they do not, no law will render them humane. We need to rethink the way they are selected for medical education, the curriculum they follow there, and the standards they are held to in practice. Nor do most children practice parricide, no matter how fraught the parent–child relationship. If they do, we may be sure that the family structure has failed, and no one can mandate its mending. We need to examine the social structure that permits human intercourse to go so dramatically awry. Part of the reason we resort to legislation for protection from our fellows is that, lacking an adequate moral education, we do not trust them to act rightly. And since they lack a moral education too, maybe our suspicions are justified! A great many of our social problems could be resolved by conversion to a belief in the essential goodness of human nature.

I'm spouting pure idealism, of course. I won't apologize, believing in the transformative power of vision, but even at the level of reality (which seems always to be characterized as grim), I'm not persuaded that we need to legalize or outlaw assisted suicide, since doing so would remove it as a site of necessary struggle. We need simply to acknowledge it as a choice that depends upon moral conviction, discuss it openly and with the gravity it deserves, trust people—patients and doctors alike—to make decisions appropriate to their own circumstances without public interference, leave them to carry these out in peace, bless those who choose to die in order to escape suffering, bless equally those who choose to live even if they suffer, let no one ever live or die without our consolation.

# Nicey Nancy and the Bad Buffaloes

ROUTE 79 from Tucson to the Arizona State Prison Complex in Florence has long been a favorite of mine, especially in springtime when paloverde and acacia burst into fountains of gold and lavender and the verges are lined with poppies and desert mallow and a particular purplish, silky grass whose name I have never learned. Although Tucson's ravening urban sprawl has swallowed great gobbets of it over the years, the stretch named the Pinal-Pioneer Parkway remains largely open desert in which someone has planted signs, at widely spaced and arbitrary intervals, labeling the vegetation. Why *this* saguaro, and not any of the hundreds just passed or the hundreds more yet to come, is anybody's guess.

Actually, until May 1999 I thought of this as the route only through, not to, Florence, the "back way" to Phoenix and its environs, quieter and more scenic than the interstate a few miles to the west. Not knowing any of the residents, I'd never thought of either the town itself or the penitentiary that provides its raison d'être as a destination. Now, however, my friend Kathy Norgard was speeding me toward a hearing before the clemency board, held on the prison grounds, where I planned to read a brief statement on behalf of Robert Wayne Vickers, an inmate on death row with whom I had corresponded for the past couple of months. Writing can certainly nudge one in queer directions. Before conceiving a book about death, although I had friends who visited prisoners, I gave little thought to following their example. Unable to explore the subject fully without pondering its unnatural aspects, however, I've become obliged to acquaint myself with murder in its various guises.

A series of excruciating events has shaped Kathy into an ideal guide, though nothing in her appearance or manner suggests that she — an affluent white psychologist in late middle age — might have any but professional connections to the world of murder and mayhem which most women like her would find unimaginable. More than twenty years ago, however, she adopted John, a fifteen-month-old boy of mixed race who would, on a September day in 1989 following his escape from a local prison, bludgeon an elderly couple to death. He wound up on death row in Florence; when a later hearing determined that his brain was too severely damaged by both genetics and fetal alcohol syndrome for him to understand his own actions, the sentence was commuted to life without parole. Thus for almost a decade Kathy has driven Route 79 back and forth on visits to John as well as for the clemency hearings and vigils that precede all Arizona executions. Just as she knows the narrow road's every bump and curve, she knows the ins and outs of the penal system.

When I wanted a pen pal on death row, then, I knew just where to turn, and Kathy put me in touch with someone who agreed to correspond with me. It was just bad luck that a warrant for his execution was issued before we'd exchanged more than a handful of letters. Today a five-member board appointed by the governor would hear arguments for and against clemency. Through the Board of Executive Clemency, which has once recommended a reprieve (although the

governor didn't grant it), the governor avoids both the pangs
of conscience (should there be any) and public criticism,
merely carrying out the experts' recommendation. Although
so used now to public speaking that I do so calmly and even
with pleasure, I felt jittery as Kathy turned off the highway,
presented our IDs at the checkpoint, drove past razor-topped
wire fences, across flat, featureless desert, and pulled into a
parking lot. As I often do when entering unfamiliar territory,
I slipped into a kind of fugue state, hyper-alert, alienated, not
at all sure I was who or where I wanted to be.

I harbored no illusions about Robert Wayne Vickers, who
occupied a cell in the heart of the heart of SMU II, the "supermax" facility opened at the Arizona State Prison Complex in
1997, a low, gray, windowless structure surrounded by a buried motion-detection cable, a microwave alarm system, and
two twenty-foot-high fences, razor wire coiled along the top
of each. The reports I'd read convinced me that he was a very
bad buffalo. He may have been a sick one, too, suffering from
temporal lobe epilepsy, which can lead to violent acts and the
failure to distinguish right from wrong, but he was denied di-
agnostic testing. Initially incarcerated for grand theft, Vickers became a murderer in 1979 when he strangled his cellmate
with a bedsheet, allegedly over a cup of Kool-Aid. Several
years later, when a fellow death-row inmate commented ob-
scenely about a photo of Vickers's niece, Vickers tossed Vi-
talis and flaming toilet paper on the man, who burned to
death. Since these acts qualify as "heinous," "cruel," and
"depraved," they certainly warranted the death penalty. If
you believe in the death penalty. George contends that this is
the one type of murderer who *does* warrant execution, the one

who poses a threat not just to society in general, from which he can be effectively removed, but to every other human being wherever he goes.

The room to which Kathy and I were directed was large and bright without being the least bit cheerful. Here during specified hours prisoners could receive visitors, but for now it held a small, subdued group. Robert himself had elected not to be present, but his aunt and sister spoke on his behalf, reciting an all too predictable catalog of abuse: a mother who hated and then abandoned him, foster homes where he was sexually molested, little education, less money, no affection. Then the victims' families were given the chance to speak. Last came those of us who had more general statements to make about the death penalty. At my turn, I said:

Just two weeks ago, the violent acts of a pair of alienated high-school students [in Littleton, Colorado] aroused people throughout the United States to paroxysms of outrage and denunciation. Politicians, pundits, and private citizens alike have blamed outside forces — among them parental negligence, the obscene lyrics of Marilyn Manson, the laxity of gun control, and the Internet — for enabling these children to act out their rageful fantasies.

These are easy accusations because, containing something of the truth, they satisfy while permitting us to stop short of the soul-searching that might lead us to the deeper understanding that our own attitudes and values are implicated. That is, what we believe, even about apparently unrelated matters, contributes to the social climate in which such atrocities take place.

Capital punishment, for example, which the majority of citizens advocate, delivers the message that execution is the generally approved means of dealing with those who have caused mortal harm. Why then do we feel surprise when children, nature's most nearly perfect imitators, put our principles into practice? We should rather be grateful that so many find other ways to deal with life's inevitable cruelties, which may seem like life-or-death issues to immature minds.

By taking lives under any circumstances whatsoever, even as retribution for unquestionably heinous acts, we poison the atmosphere in which we rear our children. Recent events make clear that we need a rapid and radical antidote. Clemency — not merely toward those whose acts are easy to forgive but toward those whose acts have hurt and horrified us deeply — can cleanse our social system in a way that killing, no matter how righteously conceived, never can. For this reason, I urge clemency today for Robert Wayne Vickers.

I returned to my place unsure whether to laugh or cry at how widely my words, with their underlying premise that executions do not secure but corrupt social well-being, had missed the mark. The people here didn't want to discuss the social morality of capital punishment, in which most of them doubtless believed, but to persuade the board to recommend taking or not taking one specific life — and viewing the matter in the light of that narrow purpose, I couldn't think of a reason Robert should be spared. If anyone deserved to die for his deeds, he did. *If . . .*

All the rest of that day and the next, Robert haunted me. Did he feel frightened? excited? relieved? Later, I would learn what he requested for his last meal. Why someone at the Arizona Department of Corrections deemed this macabre bit of information worthy of posting on the Internet, I don't know, but there you have it: green chili burritos with barbecued steak, french fries, and ketchup, vanilla ice cream, cream soda, and a cigarette. "See you later," he is reported to have said to the witnesses from the gurney to which he was strapped, and "time to go." The chemicals took two minutes to kill him.

I had lost a pen pal, but I remained on the listserv of the Coalition of Arizonans to Abolish the Death Penalty (CAADP), who sent out a request for volunteers to mail birthday cards to people on death row. Names, dates, and mailing labels would be furnished. "How hard can this be?" I asked myself, and I signed on. A lot harder than it sounded, I soon discovered. You can't just grab a card off the rack in your local drugstore, because most of them are wildly inappropriate. My favorite: "Hope you find yourself in the right place at the right time all day." The right place indeed! With some graphics software, I wound up designing and printing the cards myself for the 115 or so men and one woman then awaiting execution. "They're the scum of the earth!" one friend objected. "They don't deserve birthday cards." Maybe they didn't, but I wasn't sure it was a matter of deserts. "Someone must have loved them once," George said, imagining the promise-filled infants and toddlers they had been. After hearing the story of Robert Wayne Vickers, I was less sanguine, but perhaps someone *had* celebrated each one's coming into the world, lit one more candle on a cake each year. Chances were that the prison kitchen wasn't baking up a storm, though. No matter how monstrous his deeds, why shouldn't he be reminded that his very being had once provided an occasion for joy? Why should he—or anyone else—be required to merit so fundamental an affirmation?

To my surprise, since I hadn't thought beyond the sending, some of the first cards I sent out generated letters of thanks. I also got a telephone call from the suspicious wife of a child-murderer wanting to know who I was, as well as a vituperative note that read

> Ms. Nancy Mairs,
>     I don't know who "You Are" and I don't care who "You Are" . . . and I don't Want to Know. It's not "My Birthday." "Please, Don't Ever Do This Again" and Mined Your Own Business, and stay Out of Mine.
>                    Plain & Simple.
>                    Mr. Lopez
> P.S. You have No Right, sendin Me a Postcard. Your "Mail Is Not Accepted."

To all but the last two of these communications I replied with an offer to correspond, explaining my work on death so as to avoid any taint of exploitation. My ingenuousness doubtless amused more than one of them. *Well, of course they'll write to you,* they might have said, *so they can ask you for money.* "*I* was reluctant to write to you," one wrote recently, because "I know you write others on death row and I have heard they ask for money; I do not condone this practice and as such don't like being associated with them." He's right, some of them have asked. And really I can't blame them. If they don't have family or friends who dole out funds, they are destitute.

Locked in individual cells, which are so constructed that they can't see one another, they get little stimulation except watching television. But they have no way of generating enough income to purchase such an expensive item from the prison store, where it costs $224. Recently, a hard-labor program (suspended when an escape attempt ended with the shooting deaths of the inmate and his wife) has been reinstated, and all inmates are required to participate unless determined to be medically or mentally unfit or to present an inordinate risk to the public safety or to prison operations. For six hours every other week, wearing international-orange jumpsuits and straw hats, their hands and feet shackled, they shuffle out to tend a garden planted, one prisoner claimed to me, in defoliated earth. They are paid ten cents an hour. Small wonder they hustle bleeding-heart white ladies who send them birthday cards out of the blue and later picture postcards from Delray Beach and Denver and Boston. To them I must seem to have all the money in the world, and why shouldn't I spread it around?

In truth, if you wring my heart hard, you might get a few drops. Whether as a heritage from my Yankee forebears or a consequence of enduring a degenerative disease, I expect people to get along with having little and resign themselves to having less. The grave concerns I have about the penal system do not involve worldly goods. Indifferent to television myself, I don't consider ownership of a set an inalienable right; on the contrary, insofar as it serves to generate and inflame desire for consumable possessions and pursuits forever beyond an inmate's grasp, it might be considered an instrument of torture. Anyway, I don't feel guilty replying to an importunate letter that I don't care to have a monetary relationship. If he was simply looking for a handout, the petitioner probably won't write again. It's not as though I'm short of correspondents. Although at first I responded to each letter I received with an invitation to continue the exchange, when I got up to around a dozen, I realized that I couldn't keep track of them anymore, and the number of men from whom I hear regularly has settled at about ten. More than thirty are listed in my address book, however, so if you're looking for a pen pal . . .

"My prisoners," I call them for short, although I did not take and do not hold them. One friend objected to this locution as patronizing, not at all what I intend. It's simply a means for distinguishing my acquaintances from the more than three thousand other inmates on death rows in the thirty-eight states permitting capital punishment. Gradually, I am coming to know them a little — or at least the personas they care to present to me. Since I do not know either their family and friends from the past or the guards, chaplains, and lawyers who form their current social circle, I have no way of gauging the candor of their self-representation. I assume that, like the rest of us, they try to paint themselves in the best possible light. Nor do I know much about their crimes, about which they speak only in general terms. I have looked at them in more detail at the Arizona Department of Corrections Web site, hardly a neutral source, but I tend to forget or confuse them as soon as I stop looking. Because the crimes took place (and despite some protestations, I assume that they did take place) a long time ago, well before I "met" the perpetrators, they account for without directly influencing our interchanges. In a sense they no longer matter. My prisoners are, precisely as Sister Helen Prejean has said, dead men walking, and just how they got into that role makes less difference to me than how they now play it.

Here's the cast as I know them: LeRoy, who at eighty-five has the distinction of being the oldest death-row inmate not just in Arizona, not even in the nation, but in the world, seems to have spent most of his life in several prisons, but between one and the next he has had some grand adventures involving guns, rattlesnakes, and vast sums of money, if I am to believe the tales he spins me, and I see no reason not to. Danny, an untrained but gifted artist, works hours every day creating greeting cards (right down to the bar code on the back) from the only materials allowed him, manila folders and black ballpoint pen (and the occasional M&M for color). Donald, who punctuates his letters with smiley faces, prides himself on having saved the life of an accident victim at Graceland. Richard, a graduate of Pace University and almost my age, is a published writer, as Buddhist inmate Geo aspires to be despite his dyslexia. James's carpal tunnel syndrome renders his letters all but unreadable, but they're insightful and funny enough to reward the effort. Ron, who attended a Tucson high school for gifted students a couple of years before my daughter, also writes graceful and informative letters. Eric and Pete, by contrast, are only marginally literate. Still, Eric communicated his feelings of fear, sadness, and abandonment so vividly that George and I have begun visiting him.

Here's how I don't know them: on the lam, shooting a coin-shop employee three times during a botched robbery; bludgeoning a friend as well as the friend's grandmother and, gratuitously, his daughter in order to steal the friend's gun collection; raping and suffocating a thirteen-year-old news carrier and hiding her body in a Dumpster; shooting a wealthy homeowner in the mouth and his neighbor in the chest with exploding bullets; shooting a friend in the back of the head to get money for gambling; hired by the stepson of a wealthy socialite, shooting her five times in the head as she slept; raping at gunpoint and strangling a school chum; shooting a convenience-store clerk and a security guard in the course of a robbery; high on cocaine and alcohol, shooting the clerk in a food mart and then, at random, three women in a trailer park. These deeds are so horrific, and the circumstances leading to them so extravagantly different from my own, that I don't even know how to think about them, let alone associate them with people I know.

They are, at least in some instances, the acts of madmen, whose punishment recalls Bedlam in some eerie ways. LeRoy, like Robert Wayne Vickers, was severely abused from childhood; and knowing that such treatment devastates a child's emotional, social, intellectual, and even, on occasion, physical development, I would be surprised if the others hadn't experienced some form of it, too. Eric has told me that as long as he takes his medication, he doesn't hear the voices telling him to "kill! kill!" Ron is forthright about his paranoid schizophrenia, and at least some of the others require psychotropic drugs as well. Not by accident, I think, is the number of people on death row ten times larger today than it was before the majority of people with mental illness were, in the name of "deinstitutionalization," dumped on the streets without an adequate infrastructure to care for them. I also suspect that every one of my prisoners is addicted to some substance or behavior, to which they would return instantly if they went back on the streets.

And if they are not mad to begin with, every detail of their confinement conspires to make them that way. Like Damocles, they live always under the threat of death, often for long stretches: on average, convicts in the U.S. wait eight and a half years between sentencing and execution.* Because they can see neither each other nor the outdoors, they have no connection with the social or natural world; even the hour of exercise they are permitted three times a week takes place alone in a barren cubicle surrounded by solid walls. Those on the chain gang get out, of course, but six hours of hobbling around under the Arizona sun with a pickax in your hands doesn't encourage communion with nature or, since inmates must remain at least fifteen feet apart, your fellow man either. During the week, they may also take a fifteen-minute shower three times and make one five-minute collect phone call. They spend the rest of their time in eight-by-ten-foot cells furnished with a cot, a stool, a metal desk, an open toilet, a sink, and a stainless steel mirror, all bolted down. A seven-watt light must burn around the clock. Three times a day, an officer slides a meal through the food trap in the cell door. The food is predictably bad, they tell me, except maybe on Thanksgiving and Christmas. Those with money can supplement their diet from the prison store, but this seems to deal mostly in junky snacks and sweets. They can buy greeting cards, too, but must take what they get, and I've received some hilariously inappropriate ones. Except for books posted by bookstores, they may not receive goods from the outside but must buy them at noncompetitive prices through the store.

---

*Richard C. Dieter, Esq., "The U.S. Death Penalty and International Law: U.S. Compliance with the Torture and Race Conventions," Ford Foundation Symposium, November 12, 1998.

Alone in his cell, a prisoner may do pretty much as he likes: watch television, read, write, converse with the disembodied voices of the inmates in the cells around him or in his own head, paint murals on the walls with his excrement. The rules are as arbitrary and mutable—and nowhere near as amusing—as any Lewis Carroll could devise. According to Eric, the chaplain who brings him the Good News believes in the death penalty. Each prisoner may possess seven books, and if someone should request a bookstore to send an eighth (I made this mistake once), a guard will come in and confiscate one book at random. Their letters, both in and out, are sometimes opened and read, sometimes not. Danny may have only a black ballpoint refill for his drawings. I should think that a shank could be fashioned equally well from this as from a green or red one, but black it is. Access to the law library has been cut off. Desk lamps may be taken away, but then again, they may not. Rumors abound.

Most troubling, the inmates never come into contact with another living being. Oh, I suppose the guards may shove them from time to time, which is better than nothing, and of course they will be handled as they're strapped to a gurney and the injection site is prepared; but they will never again be touched tenderly by another human being. Nobody will kiss them goodbye. For all of us, tactile deprivation has been found to correlate with "dramatic changes in the brain's efficiency with a partial loss of memory, a lowering of the I.Q., personality changes including withdrawal, hallucinations, and in some people even an abnormal electroencephalogram," often accompanied by "depressive and autistic behaviors, hyperactivity, sexual aberration, drug abuse, violence, and aggression."* Unlike my prisoners few of us will ever experience isolation so profound as to trigger these symptoms. Examining inmates at a supermax facility in California, psychologist Craig Haney noted that many of them "experienced confused thought processes, hallucinations, irrational anger, emotional flatness, violent fantasies, social withdrawal, oversensitivity to stimuli, and chronic depression," a complex so distinctive, according to the pioneering work of Stuart Grassian, M.D., as to "form a major, clinically distinguishable psychiatric syndrome."† Already psychologically fragile, they are placed in circumstances that would drive us all right round the bend.

I tell you these things not in order to excuse my prisoners, whose deeds are inexcusable (though not therefore unforgivable), but to explain in concrete terms just what a mare's nest I have found myself in since I began communicating with them—I, the goodest of girls, who never even lifted a packet of gum from the corner drugstore, entangling myself with these baddest of boys. There are always consequences to giving an abstraction (like the death penalty) specific significance (Pete's death, now that a warrant of execution has been issued, may come quite soon). Before, despite the arguments of many abolitionist friends, I wasn't certain what I thought

---

*Robert J. Doman, M.D., "Sensory Deprivation," *Journal of the National Academy for Child Development* 4, no. 3 (1984). James W. Prescott, "Body Pleasure and the Origins of Violence," *Bulletin of the Atomic Scientists* (November 1975).

†Quoted in Sally Mann Romano, "If the SHU fits: Cruel and Unusual Punishment at California's Pelican Bay State Prison," *Emory Law Journal* (summer 1996).

about capital punishment. Although the measure didn't square with my strong pro-choice but anti-abortion stance, based on my certainty that the life of every creature (even my archenemy, the mosquito) partakes in the holy, I must admit to having felt some relief when serial killer Ted Bundy was put to death and so could never again escape to prey upon young women. I didn't see any alternative for him, and I'm still not sure that I do. My ambivalence suggested that I had an awful lot of moral work to do. I'm still at it.

I must tease out the matter of supermax facilities, for instance. You might think that since some of the inmates there are difficult and possibly dangerous even at the top of their form, prison officials and guards would want to create conditions that would minimize antisocial behaviors; but they do not. In a colossal catch-22, they incarcerate the men in maximum-security units to punish the very behaviors such incarceration will aggravate. Instead of modifying conditions, they focus on self-protection, and who can blame them? At Pelican Bay in California, writer Sally Romano reports "the totality of restraint, the presence of guards who are all clad in heavy flak jackets inside the units, the use of chains to move prisoners out of their cells, and the constant presence of control officers armed with assault rifles slung across their chests"—details suggestive of soldiers in all-out war.* Or, to be less hyperbolic, to the keeper of orangutans at the zoo. Both images would ring true for the guards, I suspect: they are locked in combat with a bunch of animals.

The inmates are as good as dead anyway, many might observe, and will be dead in fact as soon as the machinery of appeals grinds to a bitter halt, so what difference does it make whether they spend their last years rocking and babbling and

*Ibid.

picking their noses and ears like gargoyles? They're killers. They're supposed to suffer, the more horribly the better, worse than their victims suffered. Without compunction the vindictive visit their fury upon the vicious. But I don't believe that people can in good conscience employ measures designed to debase and even derange others without their cruelty redounding upon their own psyches, constricting and skewing them until they are inured to others' pain and come to excuse or even relish it. At that point, they transmogrify from custodians of lunatics or masters of beasts to tormentors, indistinguishable from their counterparts throughout history and around the globe. The fact that they employ not thumb screws, dripping water, or the rack but isolation and caprice masks but does not efface their equivalence.

Indeed, some critics contend that the treatment of inmates on death row violates the United Nations Convention against Torture and Other Cruel, Inhuman, or Degrading Treatment or Punishment, which prohibits the physical and psychological abuse of detainees throughout the world, including people who were juveniles at the time of their crime, people with mental retardation, and foreign nationals; in the United States representatives of all these categories have been executed in recent memory. In fact, in the past decade, according to Amnesty International, only five other countries executed prisoners who were under eighteen at the time of their crime: Iran, Nigeria, Pakistan, Saudi Arabia, and Yemen. Although the Torture Convention does not outlaw the death penalty itself, it provides that

pain or suffering associated with a lawful punishment can be torture if it is not closely connected with that punishment. It must arise from, or be inherent in, or incidental to a lawful sanction. If certain forms of pain and suffering can easily be avoided without eliminating the basic punishment, then it is fair to ask whether that suffering is inextricably entwined with the punishment.*

Since the protracted period of uncertainty endured by prisoners on death row is not inherent to the death penalty, the measure is arguably torturous.

So too, I would contend, many of the other conditions under which supermax inmates exist. I'm not proposing that my prisoners and their cohorts be coddled. Chances are that they belong in prison, however they may protest, and that, naturally enough, they're unhappy being there. Who wouldn't be? As inmate Pete contemplates his impending death, he writes, "This unit I am in is a hard way to live, SMU II, thier is nothing here to enjoy, so to speak of, as people on the streets would call enjoyment." At the bleakness in his words, I feel sad but neither guilty nor outraged, as I would if his human rights were being violated. In one coked-up frenzy, Pete separated himself from "people on the street" and forfeited what they enjoy. As far as I'm concerned, the inmates can live like Spartans, as long as they have ample natural light, wholesome food, fresh air, and the opportunity for social intercourse.

Believing firmly in the civilizing effects of literacy, I would give them as many books as they wanted and encourage them to continue their education. I would make sure they had ample access to spiritual (not necessarily Christian) guides who, conversant with and committed to the concepts and

---

*Dieter, "U.S. Death Penalty," op. cit.

practices of reconciliation and restoration, can help them deal with the anguish they have given others and themselves. I would stop the stupid make-work of the chain gang and set them about some serious gardening, so that they can help provide for themselves, and other productive tasks as well. I would also encourage creative pursuits like Richard's, Geo's, and Danny's by permitting them the materials they need. If letting Danny have more than one pen is too dangerous, I'd at least let him trade it for a different color from time to time. And if they could earn money from their efforts, so much the better.

If I were planning to kill them, as poll after poll suggests that two-thirds of U.S. residents would do, I would act as soon after their sentencing as possible to spare them years of tedium and false hope. And I would require that a group of citizens — say twelve, the number considered sufficient to condemn them — be selected by lot and required no more than once to witness their executions, which are now carried out at an all but hermetic remove from ordinary human activity. As a society, we too eagerly divorce the beliefs we hold and the measures enacted (by others acting on our behalf) to give them force from the reality those measures effect. Most of the anti-choice demonstrators outside a family-planning clinic won't stick around to see the child they've "rescued" sodomized by his mother's new boyfriend at three, beaten bloody by her *new* new boyfriend at eight, smoking crystal meth at twelve, dropping out of school at fifteen, shooting a liquor-store clerk through the heart at twenty-two. Few of those demanding that the police get the homeless off the streets will ride the bus with them to an overcrowded shelter for a meal featuring day-old bread and tinned peaches followed by a few restless hours wrapped in a scratchy blanket on a canvas cot, dreading the thrust of a penis in the anus or a blade between the ribs. More than likely, the woman I heard on television dismissing the death penalty as "cleaning house" pays someone else to clean her own house.

In short, we avoid any activity we view as likely to distress us. And many of us appear to find death more distressing than any other element of existence. Since we send even those we love away to be tended and later to be prepared for burial by strangers, we aren't likely to keep watch outside an execution chamber. But we aren't responsible for the deaths of those we love (or, if we are, we'll wind up in the execution chamber), whereas we are, through accepting our role as law-abiding citizens, collectively accountable for deaths mandated by the state, whether or not we believe individually in capital punishment. Ethical authenticity forbids us from turning our faces away from a law's consequences simply because we don't like the view. Those whom we would kill demand our witness.

Given my druthers, I would not kill murderers at all, however, but sentence them to life in prison without parole (the proportion of death-penalty advocates drops to about half when this option is given). With my horror of enclosure, I don't think I'd be doing them any favor. The fact that proponents of capital punishment consider any measure short of execution to be too lenient reflects the dread with which they view death rather than any insight into the ends and efficacy of various means of punishment. To lose the world and "live" for years in confinement with the memory and consequence of their deeds strikes me as the harsher fate. I find myself hard-pressed to defend it.

But defend it I must, since I can think of no sound reason for killing yet another person which might outweigh the social and spiritual costs such a measure exacts. Prevention? As anyone who's ever trained a dog soon learns, fear of punishment is a weak deterrent at best, and I suspect that the interior tumult leading to/aroused by murderous intent and action tends to eclipse it altogether. I try to imagine Eric lowering the security guard's .357 revolver from the Short Stop clerk's ashen face with the thought, "Uh-uh. Mustn't do. Could fry for this." A cruel, depraved, and heinous murder is unlikely to be perpetrated by someone who (a) has thought of the death penalty at all before acting or (b), if he has pondered the punishment, has considered the possibility that *he* might get caught and sentenced to die. Like the murder that may lead to it, capital punishment seems a fate that befalls some unknown other, certainly not your precious and perdurable self.

Not deterrence, then. Vengeance? "An eye for an eye," the righteous intone, invoking Mosaic law, which, like the Code of Hammurabi before it, served not so much to condone as to restrain retribution by requiring that the punishment not exceed the crime; now, however, we think of it as prescribing rather than moderating our responses to transgression. "Anyone who deprives someone else of life," my daughter tells me succinctly, "loses the right to live." No rough justice here, but an economy of arithmetical exactitude: whatever you take from me, for good or ill, I get the equivalent back from you. This equation works pretty well if, say, you have stolen my

automobile, since you must give me another automobile of
the same value in recompense, and so we both still have
wheels (although nowadays, oddly, you are likely to land in
jail instead, and then you won't have any use for wheels,
whereas, unless my vehicle is recovered, I won't have any
wheels to use).

The logic of *lex talionis*—"life for life, eye for eye, tooth
for tooth, hand for hand, foot for foot" (Deuteronomy
19:21)—breaks down as soon as the terms involve something
other than simple property, which can be replaced by its exact
equivalent. Suppose I splash acid into your eyes. To punish
my nefarious act, you are entitled to put my eyes out, too; indeed, some would argue that you are required to do so lest
eye-putting-out become a social epidemic. Still, the loss of
my vision won't restore yours. Instead of one blind person,
we'll have two, an impractical outcome, it seems to me, both
of us stumbling about in the dark when one could have been
leading the other. In the same way, if you kill someone whom
I love, I may insist that you be killed in revenge. Since my beloved will not return to me once you are dead, I must take my
satisfaction from the fact that where initially there was one
dead person, now there are two, a source of contentment so
peculiar that I shiver at the thought. Even though the two
deaths differ, the murder unlawful and the execution sanc-
tioned by Arizona and thirty-seven other states, I do not want
to be heartened by anybody's demise. Oh, but you'd feel
differently if it happened to you, proponents of capital punishment have told me, and I could only wonder whether they
were right, whether I was being idealistic or ingenuous,
whether a vindictive thirst would well up in me which could

be slaked only by blood. Now it has happened to me, and I don't feel differently at all, except perhaps that I find capital punishment more puzzling than ever. Crushed by my loss, how could I wish for *more* death?

"You have heard that it was said, 'An eye for an eye and a tooth for a tooth,'" declares the Jesus of the Gospels. "But . . ." Ah yes, the almighty *but* that prefaces his prescriptions for a radically new way of structuring human interaction. In this passage (Matthew 5:38–45) he turns retaliation on its head. Instead of exacting recompense for injuries, we are instructed to incur more: smitten cheeks, nakedness, wearying travels, depletion of resources. Biblical commentators tend to apologize all too quickly for Jesus' loonier injunctions, assuring us that he didn't intend to be taken literally but merely to illustrate a heavenly ideal, that of course we must still punish muggers, thieves, and deadbeats if such people aren't to get away with, you should excuse the expression, murder. Otherwise, the entire social order will come crashing down around our ears and we won't be safe in our own beds. In truth, however, retaliation, by fostering aggrievedness on the one hand and triumphalism on the other, sickens social intercourse, which can best be restored by the proactive generosity Jesus recommends. I think he means for us to follow his instructions.

Even more impossibly, Jesus insists that we *love* our afflicters if we are to be the children of God, who "makes his sun rise on the evil and on the good, and sends rain on the just and on the unjust," a point commentators prefer to skip over—not this time because Jesus sounds otherworldly, I think, but because he has grasped a discomforting reality of this world: that all people may receive life's fundamental blessing, love, whether they deserve it or not. Grace, not fairness, is the principle on which the holy rests and toward which Jesus adjures us to strive. Between Nicey Nancy and the Bad Buffaloes of death row God does not choose. Not that God can't distinguish between us, good and evil, just and unjust (and God knows who is which). Not that God condones the wickedness and cruelty with which my prisoners and their confreres have acted. But she does forgive, which is an altogether sterner and more rigorous process, reconciling us to herself, pouring out her gratuitous love on every one. For God, death is not a penalty inflicted upon her creatures but an infolding of our sorry selves into the All that is our source and destination. This mysterious embrace lies well beyond any human fathoming, and we do well to meet it on its own terms, not our own. Donald, James, Ron, Danny, Geo, LeRoy, Richard, Eric, and Pete have all transgressed more appallingly than they, their victims, and their would-be executioners know. We may—must—remove them from our midst and help them atone in whatever natural span they have left. Their deaths do not belong to us.

# Ron Her Son: Coda

"MY son has been murdered," the voice in my ears says into the telephone, "and I need to make arrangements for his body."

Whose voice speaks these words? And what on earth is she talking about?

Almost twenty years ago, I wrote an essay titled "Ron Her Son" about the experience of taking in an adolescent boy whom my husband had met while teaching at a school for emotionally disturbed children, an experience that I would not have missed—and would not repeat—for all the world. The out-of-wedlock child of an alcoholic Athabaskan woman and a soldier at Fort Yukon, Ron had been given away by or taken away from his mother (the story is complicated, and no two tellers narrate quite the same details) at age one and grew up in two non-Native foster families before ours. By the time we met him, he was sullen and wary, clearly expecting us to hand him along to someone else before long. We never did, though God knows I was tempted. Recently, I learned that he considered his life to have begun when he came to live with us.

Although I recall those years as joyless, he—like the others in the family—was more the victim than the cause of my woes, which sprang from untreated depression and my steadily worsening MS. In fact, most of the problems Ron presented in his peculiarly stony fashion—which I ascribed to the fact that because he had been abandoned by one parental figure after another, he was academically delayed and emotionally disturbed—turned out, I discovered ten years later when my son Matthew reached the same age, to be merely symptoms of male adolescence. We all struggled, and often floundered, through our years together; we all survived. In thus becoming our third, though oldest, child, Ron caused us to revise our concept of "family" so radically that now all the world's children belong to us. We just haven't met some of them yet. And I certainly hope they don't all come to live with us.

At the time I wrote that essay Ron had graduated from high school and left to join the navy, where he was trained as a radioman. Having married a young woman named Angel and fathered two little boys, Alex and Chris, he had brought them home for their first visit, an event that I found profoundly moving because, through it, Ron laid claim to us as ordinary—and permanent—parents and grandparents. Because, from her point of view, we were ordinary in-laws, Angel sent letters and photos faithfully. Even though over the next decade or so, bouncing among duty stations on the East Coast and in Iceland, they visited only once more, we felt very much a part of their lives. These were not easy. Alex suffered from ear infections and Chris was accident-prone; their vehicles were forever breaking down; they were chronically short of money; Ron drank more and more heavily; more than once Angel took the boys and went home to her mother in Texas. Ron must have prized his family above all else, because in spite of his genetic heritage he stopped drinking and got them back.

After he had served seventeen years, the navy offered Ron $40,000 if he would leave before retirement. Well, maybe "offered" is too polite a term. The military was scaling back and wanted higher ranking (and therefore higher paid) personnel to leave. If he didn't take the offer, he was told, he might be let go at any time without compensation. I suppose $40,000 sounded like a lot of money, though it was a pittance compared to what his retirement might have brought him. He took it and, to our delight, the family moved to Tucson in 1993. The money was gone in a year, but by then Ron had a good job, with benefits, maintaining the surveillance equipment used for security at the casino run by the Tohono O'odham tribe south of the city.

In other ways, their lives continued to be difficult. The troubled relationship between Ron and Chris deteriorated further as Chris approached adolescence. Once again, Angel took the boys back to Waco, and this time they were gone for a year. When they returned, the boys did not do well. They both dropped out of school, and Chris had some run-ins with the law. Both produced out-of-wedlock daughters. Eventually, Alex found a low-level but steady job and moved to Phoenix. Chris worked now and then. He moved out of the house. Angel and Ron seemed to like their new freedom. They bought a mobile home and adopted a little dog they named Duchess. "We were happy," Angel told me. "At last we were happy. We even talked about taking the honeymoon we never had."

At 6:35 on the morning of August 24, 2000, Angel called and told George that Ron had been shot. If she gave him any details, he was too sleepy to take them in. He hastily got me up and dressed, and we set off for the University Medical Center, just a couple of blocks from our back door. The room number Angel had given was in the intensive care unit. We were admitted immediately. Outside Ron's room a nurse stopped us. "He's been shot in the head," she warned, "and his condition is very poor." She made room among the machines for my wheelchair to approach the bed.

Ron was both there and not there. Naked under a sheet, he lay on his back with his arms at his sides, an almost regimental pose. Tubes snaked under his moustache, through his lips, and down his throat. Through one, a breath was forced into his lungs every few seconds, making his chest heave in a simulacrum of liveliness. A bright blue bandage swaddled his skull. Below it, his eyes, though slightly open, saw nothing. I don't think either of us doubted that our Ron was already gone, leaving this barely recognizable husk, to which we instinctively reached out, murmuring, "We love you." We had spoken these words to him from time to time over the years. Recently, at least once, he had responded, "I love you, too."

In the visitors' lounge we found Angel, accompanied by a Victim Witness advocate and the hospital chaplain, and learned from her what had happened. Ron had kissed her goodnight and gone to bed, leaving her to finish the television program she was watching. Without locking the doors, she'd drifted off. She came to when someone grabbed her by the hair and hauled her off the couch, across the room, and into the hall. The bedroom door was ajar. She couldn't see anything, but she heard someone shout, "Ernesto wants his money!" A shot. Ron's voice: "Ow! Ow!" Another shot. The intruders—two men between eighteen and twenty—stood

over Angel arguing with each other in Spanish. Were they
trying to decide whether to kill her, too? In English they demanded the key to Ron's truck, but when she told them it
wasn't working, they took her car instead. She fainted. When
she came to some time later, she found Ron lying in the bath-
room and called 911.

We couldn't make sense of the story then or anytime later.
Who could these young men have been, and what were they
after? Surely not a white Ford Escort in such poor mechanical
condition that they ditched it, or it ditched them, just a few
blocks away. Ron and Angel's mobile home had been burgla-
rized a couple of weeks earlier, and Ron's handgun had been
taken. Could the two crimes be connected—and if so, how?
Possibly the intruders struck randomly. Or they'd mistaken
Ron for someone else. Angel said she and Ron didn't know
anyone named Ernesto. Unless Ron led some sort of secret
life. Unless they were after Chris, who'd gotten at least casually involved in the local drug scene. Over time, and in the
wee hours, our speculations sometimes grew wild. At one
point I caught myself imagining that I was responsible because I was working on a book of essays about death.

George and I went down to the cafeteria to get a little
breakfast. For various reasons I have spent a good bit of time
there, so that although it is hardly as comfortable as my own
dining room, it is nearly as familiar. Suddenly, however, it
seemed altered, alien, and I felt for the first time a shift that
has haunted me since. I was not the woman who had come
there before. The clerk in Java City made me a latte, took my
money, as though I were a norm⸍ person. But I had turned
into something quite different: the mother of a murdered
child. Except in nightmares your children don't die, I kept

telling myself. And they certainly don't get shot. That's the stuff of detective novels and television shows. It's not *real*. It is real. I know that. For years I have had a friend, Bill, whose daughter was abducted from a parking lot, driven in her own car into the desert, and raped before being killed. Still, despite my sympathy for Bill, he had remained the other, the parent to whom the unthinkable had happened, his grief beyond imagination. Now I am that other.

While we were gone, the neurologist had spoken to Angel. "He's not going to make it," she sobbed, confirming our initial impression. "There's nothing they can do." Later, we learned that the doctors in the emergency room had taken a look and then bandaged his head to hold his brain in. There wasn't even anything they could *try* to do. He had been put on life support until we could be consulted about organ donation. Now two nurses took us into a conference room and opened the discussion. Yes, Angel said, she and Ron had talked from time to time over the years about donating their organs after death, and he seemed to favor the idea as much as she did, but she really didn't know much about it. Her eyes widened when she was told that as many as five hundred people could benefit, not just from internal organs like his kidneys and liver but from tissues, tendons, valves, corneas, and the like. His death might seem less of a waste if others were leading better lives because of it.

The process was hedged about with safeguards so that it couldn't be called into ethical question. Ron would have to be pronounced "brain dead," a determination that required the absence of reflexive response to a series of stimuli, such as a tug on his arms or ice water poured into his ear. The final test would be the cessation of breath when the ventilator was turned off. Brain death would be brought about by pressure downward on the brain stem as the traumatized brain swelled ever larger inside his skull. Throughout, they assured us, he would—could—feel nothing. Although the timing couldn't be precise, they estimated that he might die by afternoon. At the instant he was pronounced dead, his body would be rushed to the operating room so that removal of the organs could begin. With Angel's permission and our support, he had become what is known in the trade as a "harvest."

In the end, we wished that they hadn't made any prediction, since this scenario didn't play out as it was supposed to do. With Angel we went back to our house, expecting all afternoon a telephone call from the ICU. At dinnertime, we called and Ron's nurse told us that his condition hadn't changed. In the evening Angel drove to the airport to pick up her mother, Beryl. While I waited at home to greet her and settle the two of them in, George went back to the hospital to sit with Ron, whose condition remained the same, George reported on his return. George was taken with the way the ICU staff treated Ron—turning him gently, rubbing lotion into his back, patting his shoulder, calling him by name, just as though he were really there. And truly something was still there, a somatic Ron, essential, Ron in every cell, even in the absence of the cortical functions we associate with personhood.

In the morning there was still no change. Months before, I had agreed to read at a conference on medicine, ethics, and the humanities in a town about a four-hour drive north of Tucson, and we decided to honor the commitment. Before setting out in the afternoon, we stopped in to see Ron. When his nurse said that he seemed no closer to death than he had the day before, my breath caught in my throat.

"How long is this going to take?" I asked. She immediately dropped to her haunches in front of my wheelchair and took my hands.

"We don't know," she said. "It can sometimes take days." A far cry from the few hours originally forecast. The problem, she explained, was that the exit wound was so large that the brain was swelling outward through it instead of pressing downward as anticipated.

"We're not talking something like a persistent vegetative state here, are we?" I asked, recalling the ordeal of a friend whose husband, revived after a massive coronary, had spent more than a year lying comatose in a nursing home before his death. No, she assured me, nothing like that. We would be given the option of withdrawing life support. And though it might take a while, Ron would doubtless die without the ventilator and intravenous nutrition. In this case, however, his would be a "cardiac death" rather than a "brain death," and his organs could not be donated. (Ironically, the hospital would alter this policy less than two weeks later.)

George and I sat by Ron's bed for a while. Someone had put a hospital gown over his bare chest, I was glad to see. He'd been modest. His eyes were now shut, so that he appeared to be at rest. "You can go now, Ron," I said to him. "Angel is very sad, but she'll be okay. The boys will be okay. You've done everything you need to do. Go quickly now. Go in peace." Then we sang him the lullaby my family has sung to its infants ever since I can remember.

*Sleep, baby, sleep.*
*Our cottage vale is deep.*
*The little lamb is on the green,*
*With woolly fleece so soft and clean.*
*Sleep, baby, sleep.*

We left praying—oh, the inner turmoil of hoping for the death of someone you love!—that we would not see him again.

Accustomed to traveling for some distance, sleeping in unfamiliar beds, spending anything from a few hours to several days with people we are unlikely ever to see again (conditions that lead to a sense of dream and drift even when we're not distracted), we got through the conference smoothly enough. I read "Sex and Death and the Crippled Body" to about a hundred nurses and doctors. Raising end-of-life issues, the essay was begun as an ethical exercise. Perhaps in ignorance I was rehearsing for this eerie state, where the political has become personal, into which an intruder with a pistol has thrown me.

I wanted someone to hasten my son's death, finish off what that pistol began. He was not suffering, they insisted, but how could they know for sure? Perhaps at some level no monitor could measure, that mutilated brain was shrieking. And what about us, gazing into his blank face, stroking his inert limbs? Did our anguish not count for something? He would have hated to grieve us so. He would have wanted us to release him. This matter has continued to perplex me. Although I recognize the potential for abuse if survivors were granted wholesale legal permission to request euthanasia for a dying "loved one," I believe that such a decision could be made case by case. In ours, no one doubted that Ron was going to die—was, in effect, dead already—nor did any of us stand to profit by his doing so sooner rather than later. And the chances that an entire bioethics committee would be so corrupt as to support a dubious demand strike me as vanishingly remote.

Knowing that we'd be weary at the end of the conference, we had planned on staying another night before heading home, but under the circumstances relaxation seemed impossible. We were back in Tucson by 7:30 that evening.

Ron's sister, Mary, and her son, Randy, had arrived. Mary's appearance in Ron's life five years ago was—I don't know any other way to put it—purely a blessing. They shared the same mother and, six years his senior, Mary had known him as a baby. She gave him a picture of himself with his first birthday cake. I've got a picture of myself with my first birthday cake. Chances are you do, too. I have pictures of my mother and father, the houses we lived in, the pets who lived with us. I have a whole repertoire of stories about myself dating from before my earliest memories: Boo (they called me) seizing a fallen tomato and screwing up her face at its unexpected sourness; Boo peering into the toilet after a dropped plaything and tutting, "Honey Miff, how cou-choo, how cou-choo?" Through their tales—augmented technologically these days not just by snapshots but by videotape—the adults in our lives remember us into being: who we are, what kind of world we inhabit, how we fit among those around us in that world.

Ron had no such sense of his origins until Mary found him. Married and with two grown boys of her own, Mary had never forgotten "little Roddy." (He had first been named Elwood Roderick Gabriel or Rose, even his name unstable, de-fying him to form an identity.) Their mother, having been told that he'd been adopted and was living happily in Texas and that if she tried to find him, she'd ruin his new life, for-bade Mary to search for him. Her prohibition died with her, however, and before long Ron had a letter from the tribe in-forming him about a sister he never knew he had. Ron had the flattest affect of anyone I have ever known, but he seemed happy at this news, happy and rather self-important, as though having a sister conferred a self to feel important with. When she arrived for a visit, he came close to strutting.

Although they had different fathers, hers Athabaskan and his white, he could see something of himself when he looked into her beautiful face, with its wide-set dark eyes and promi-nent cheekbones. She brought him beadwork their mother had done and snapshots of her and other relatives. She told him that their mother had always remembered Roddy and longed for him. She reminisced about the short time he had lived with them, how when her father got drunk and beat her mother, she grabbed Roddy and they hid in a closet and later ran through the dark to an aunt's house, she could still feel his little hand in hers as he struggled to keep up.

After Mary went home, she sent him an album of photos with a short family history that resonated with the same sort of memories: of poverty, rage, brutality, alcoholism, abuse. "Oh Ron," I said when I'd finished reading it, "I don't know . . ."

"Yeah," he said, "maybe I was lucky I left there." We had all always assumed that Ron had had the rottenest possible childhood, being separated from his birth mother and shunted from one family to another, never putting down any but the shallowest roots, never really taking hold and flourishing. But as far as we could tell, his foster mother Mary Du-Gay had loved him. He had always had enough to eat. There was a bicycle and even a pony. Despite grave deficiencies, he graduated from high school, did well in the navy, held a responsible civilian job, stayed with and supported his family, and overcame his dependency on alcohol. He was hell to live with, emotionally unavailable, sullen, hot-tempered, and verbally abusive, and his own children have paid a high price for their paternity; but he was remarkably functional. He had come to his first foster family malnourished and covered with sores. If he had lived to adulthood, chances are he would not have prospered.

We all agreed — Ron's wife, his sons, his parents, his sister — that Ron had lingered in life-support limbo long enough. His brain, though it had oozed from his ears and nostrils and pushed one of his eyes forward in its socket, still hadn't compressed the brain stem. Whether or not he was actually suffering, we perceived his heaving chest and staring eye as signs of distress. He might not still be "there," but he wasn't dead either. Though we were sorry to waste his organs, we needed resolution.

Come in when you're ready, Angel had been told, and a doctor will sign the order for stopping the ventilator and IV fluids. By 10:30 on Sunday morning, we were gathered in the visitors' lounge. Alex couldn't bear to come at all. Chris came for a while but couldn't bring himself to stay. Mary, Randy, and Beryl planned to wait in the lounge. Angel, George, and I would be with Ron when life support was removed.

George went in to let the ICU staff know we were ready and returned with the report that the attending neurosurgeon wouldn't be in until 11:00. We filled the half-hour with a listless trip to the cafeteria. At 11:00, the doctor had still not arrived. The lounge was occupied by three or maybe four generations of an enormous family. We clustered in the corridor, our faces wan under the fluorescent lighting, our gestures restless. Other, similar groups were scattered up and down the hall.

At 11:45, I stomped into the ICU. "This is unacceptable," I said to Sheri, Ron's nurse, and the young resident standing with her. "We've been waiting almost an hour and a half. His wife is suffering. We're all suffering." They looked appalled and apologetic. The doctor was in the hospital, they told me, but he wasn't responding to their pages. There was nothing more they could do. At last, while we were talking, he bustled in, trailing a medical student whom he did not introduce. Without apology he directed that we be assembled in the conference room. There, he went over the details of Ron's condition with which we were now so familiar—more familiar, I suspect, than he was, since he didn't appear to have seen Ron since the emergency room. He went on to warn that if we ordered life support withdrawn and Ron's killer were later caught, his lawyer could claim his innocence because Ron had technically been alive until that point. He wouldn't have "killed" Ron, we would.

"I wanted to say to him, 'Gee, I never thought of that,'" Angel said to me later, "'and who the fuck cares?'" I wish she had. I wish one of us had challenged his insensitivity instead of listening, mouths all but hanging open, while he strutted his neurological and legal stuff. I wish someone had said to the student soaking up his words, "Here is a lesson in the very worst way to approach a family who has asked that treatment be terminated." He asked us few questions, none open-ended. He revealed no awareness of the moral and emotional labor that had occupied us for more than three days. Until he had spoken, his attitude suggested, we couldn't possibly reach a rational decision. But we no longer needed his cautions. We needed his signature. I wanted to sympathize with the under-lying distress (dread of death? hatred of failure? anxiety that one of us might burst out howling at any moment?) that must be fueling his aloof arrogance, but I was fresh out of patience.

Once we had the signature, the process began almost immediately. At about 1:00, with George, Angel, and I at the bedside, the ventilator and IV lines were detached and Ron began to breathe on his own. Shortly, Angel shook her head and said, "I can't do this. I can't watch him die." We urged her to collect the others and wait at home. After getting some lunch in the cafeteria, George and I settled beside Ron. He continued to breathe, keeping the level of oxygen in his blood high. "This may take quite a while," Sheri predicted. With mountains of schoolwork on his desk, George decided to go home for a while.

I needed to stay. I couldn't explain why. I knew that my Ron had died days before. With his pulverized and swollen brain he couldn't experience the sense of strangulation my mother had so feared, Sheri promised me, and if he exhibited the least sign of discomfort, she would administer morphine. But he never moved. He couldn't possibly know that I sat there, not in any way I would recognize as "knowing." Yet I couldn't bear that even his body die alone. Also, having sat by my mother and stepfather as each died, I knew the sense of closure such witness could confer. Perhaps I kept watch as much for my own sake as for Ron's.

He kept breathing at a steady rate for the next couple of hours. Then some friends came in and, although I'd have preferred to continue my contemplative vigil, as my Garmie's granddaughter I rose to the social occasion. Members of Community of Christ of the Desert, the small faith community in which I worship, they clearly intended to bring me comfort, and I was touched. Engaged in conversation, I found it hard to attend to Ron's progress. At one point, when bloody saliva trickled from his mouth, I did excuse myself and find someone to mop it up. And Sheri faithfully came in to tell me of changes she observed. His breathing slowed to about half its original rate. His blood oxygen dropped. To compensate, his blood pressure rose steeply. Finally, she said, "I don't think it will be very long now. You might want to call your husband."

In the midst of preparing supper, he promised to come as soon as he could. My friends offered to stay until he arrived, clearly believing that I shouldn't be alone at such a moment, but I urged them to go along. I was not alone. Ron was there. And I wanted to concentrate on the mysterious transition now taking place, not altogether easily. At forty-one Ron was in basically good health. Cigarettes and animal fat would have caught up with him eventually—had there been any "eventually"—but at this point he was vigorous. His body struggled to survive. "Don't ever think he left you lightly," I said to Angel later. "Even after he stopped breathing and he was getting no more oxygen, his heart kept beating." But not for long, of course. The line on the monitor went flat. The young resident, who had been as attentive as the neurosurgeon was negligent, pressed her stethoscope to Ron's heart and pronounced him dead at 6:10 P.M. on August 27. Although this became the official date of Ron's demise, we still think of him as having died on August 24. What followed was not life, and with time, we hope those surreal intervening days will fade from memory.

I sat with him until George arrived a few minutes later. The body would be sent to the medical examiner, from whom the mortuary we chose could claim it for cremation. Nothing remained for us to do except to remove the silver chain Ron always wore around his neck. "Let me do that," Sheri said when George started to lift Ron's head; later he realized that she had wanted to make sure Ron's brain didn't spill from his skull, and he was grateful. He undid the clasp and cupped the chain. We walked the couple of blocks home through a lurid sunset and the tantalizing whiff of rain.

And so it was indeed my own voice I heard on the telephone talking to the funeral director about my murdered child. Once a date was set, Angel, George, and I sketched a plan for a service in celebration of Ron's life, which George would conduct. We'd learned from Mother's service that unless the dead one and/or the family has had a relationship with a particular minister or similar figure, the family is likely to do the livelier (excuse the expression) job of evoking a sense of the specific character and value of the person who now resides solely in their memories. Ron hadn't wanted a service at all, a wish we did not choose to honor; but we could keep the pro-

ceedings brief, simple, and—since he was an adamant athe-
ist—nonreligious. Angel went off to procure a Marvin the
Martian cookie jar to hold Ron's ashes and some Jelly Bellies,
his favorite candy, to share with the mourners. George set
about composing his remarks. I wrote an obituary and designed a pamphlet for the service. We bought a little recorder
and a tall white candle. Our plans and errands enabled us to
begin turning away from the horrific images of Ron in the
past few days to memories of the living boy and man.

This desire to mourn Ron's loss without dwelling on the
manner of his death may fuel the ambivalence we seem to
share about the police investigation that continues. "Don't
you want to know what really happened?" people ask, and of
course we do. There seems to be little evidence, though, and
the police force is stretched thin in this violent city. Since the
killers could act again, we'd like them caught and imprisoned
for society's sake—but not our own. We know from talking
to people in Homicide Survivors that catching and punishing
them won't lessen our grief. In fact, under the current legal
system, victims' families can find themselves pulled back into
court repeatedly, a little wearier each time, a little bitterer,
their healing hearts lacerated anew by the killer's face, the re-
iteration of details, the suspicion that they are pawns in a law-
yerly game of one-upmanship. And so we find ourselves half
hoping that we will be allowed to go free, even if "justice"
doesn't get done.

"It seems so unfair that the story should end like this," a
friend wrote after learning of Ron's death and rereading "Ron
Her Son." All catastrophes seem unfair, one might fairly argue. But I know just what she means. Perhaps there is a larger

pattern into which Ron's death fits snugly as into a well-wrought puzzle—and I believe there is, calling the puzzle God—but I cannot discern it. In my human judgment, an injustice has been done. Having struggled through an unusually painful childhood, having escaped madness, addiction, and prison—the likeliest outcomes of such a beginning—having achieved a measure of stability and even success none of us could have predicted, Ron seemed to merit something more than a bullet through the brain. Having worked through the marital problems engendered by his volatile silences and explosions, Angel deserved many more of the companionable hours they'd started to spend sitting on the porch with the dog, smoking cigarettes and chatting. Damaged by a father whose absences, often physical, always emotional, were interrupted only by menacing rage, the boys needed to emerge into adulthood if they were ever to understand Ron's limitations and temper their hatred with pity. There were signs that the tone of Ron's story was brightening. I wish he'd lived further into the happy part.

No matter how unjustly, Ron's story ceases here. But our stories do not. In them, Ron's death figures as an element, not an end, and we don't know yet how that element will function in the plot once we are no longer stunned and stupid with grief. Ron's death could mark the upward turn. Maybe, after twenty-two years in a marriage she intermittently struggled to escape, Angel will flourish in her new independence. Perhaps, once the ogre their childish psyches made of their father no longer looms, the boys will find less combative ways of relating to the world and begin to live responsibly as the men their bodies are turning them into. Plenty of less sunny scenarios clamor to suggest themselves, but I elect to ignore them. Just now I need comfort, not clear vision. As for George and me, our circumstances are unlikely to change dramatically. But our interior lives have once again deepened and saddened in a way we can hope will lead us toward wisdom. However the details work themselves out, all our stories will always hold the mute and meaningless fact of Ron's murder, and we will learn to live with it.

The end. For now.

# Resources

The profusion of material dealing with death and the rapidity with which it proliferates guarantee that no single person could ever absorb it all. That is my temptation whenever I begin a project: to track down every scrap ever produced dealing even tangentially with my subject and gobble it all up with the plan of transforming the mass into a substantial book. Well, it's true that whatever we devour gets transformed, but unless I want to produce literary turds, that's just the wrong way to go about writing a book and not just a digest-of-great-thoughts-anybody-has-ever-had-about-subject-X. First you've got to find out what you think about subject X, I remind myself; your thoughts may be wrongheaded or silly, but at least they're *yours*.

Nevertheless, nobody ever thinks in a vacuum, and so my work is bound to be informed in some way or other by my encounters with the ideas of others. In a sweeping sense, these would include every book or article I've read, every film or television program I've watched, every discussion I've held on the subject in question. At my age, there are many too many of these, most of them forgotten or badly remembered, either for me to catalog them or for anyone else to get much use out of the catalog. Included here is a highly selective list of materials that I've come across at some point and found fruitful in themselves and/or as guides to further resources, beginning — as I always begin — with books.

Byock, Ira. *Dying Well: The Prospect of Growth at the End of Life.* New York: Putnam/Riverhead, 1997.

De Hennezel, Marie. *Intimate Death: How the Dying Teach Us How to Live.* New York: Knopf, 1997.

Johnson, Fenton. *Geography of the Heart: A Memoir.* New York: Scribner, 1996.

Kübler-Ross, Elisabeth. *On Death and Dying.* 1969; reprint, New York: Scribner Classics, 1997.

Mitford, Jessica. *The American Way of Death.* New York: Simon & Schuster, 1963.

Nuland, Sherwin B. *How We Die: Reflections on Life's Final Chapter.* New York: Knopf, 1994.

Rinpoche, Sogyal. *The Tibetan Book of Living and Dying.* San Francisco: Harper, 1992.

Rose, Gillian. *Love's Work: A Reckoning with Life.* New York: Schocken, 1997.

Rothman, J. C. *Saying Goodbye to Daniel: When Death Is the Best Choice.* New York: Continuum, 1995.

Shulman, Alix Kates. *A Good Enough Daughter.* New York: Schocken, 1999.

Sontag, Susan. *Illness as Metaphor and AIDS and Its Metaphors.* New York: Anchor/Doubleday, 1990.

Webb, Marilyn. *The Good Death: The New American Search to Reshape the End of Life.* New York: Bantam, 1997.

Williams, Terry Tempest. *Refuge: An Unnatural History of Family and Place.* New York: Vintage, 1991.

Because of the sheer volume of undigested stuff it contains, the Internet tends to be a clumsy research tool. But if you're

willing to bumble about, you can find well-constructed, substantial sites, which are often linked to other, similar sites. A
bumbler by nature, I've turned up a wealth of information.
Here are a few death-specific Web sites worth visiting:

Death Penalty Information Center:
www.deathpenaltyinfo.org

Dying Well: www.dyingwell.org

Kearl's Sociology of Death and Dying:
www.trinity.edu/mkearl/death.html

Last Acts: www.lastacts.org

Pro-Death Penalty: www.prodeathpenalty.com

Project on Death in America, Soros Foundation:
www.soros.org/death.html

Robert Wood Johnson Foundation: www.rwjf.org

Although my responses to death have been enriched by
audio and video productions too numerous to mention, a few
have worked on me with particular power. These include Bill
Moyers's television series *On Our Own Terms;* Lou Reed's album *Magic and Loss;* Errol Morris's documentary *Mr. Death:
The Rise and Fall of Fred A. Leuchter, Jr.;* and the films *The
Winter Guest*, directed by Alan Rickman, and *Dead Man*, directed by Jim Jarmusch.